W9-AAX-264

Born in 1940 Larissa Miller was educated at the Foreign Languages Institute in Moscow and later taught at Moscow University. A major lyrical poet, she is the author of ten books, including *Nameless Day*; *My Land and Home*; *Let's Talk about the Paradoxes of Love*; *Holidays, Holidays*; *Between the Cloud and the Pit*.

Winner of several literary prizes she was short-listed for the State Prize in 2000.

In *Dim and Distant Days*, Miller looks back over nearly five decades of Soviet history to her hungry but happy childhood in post-war Moscow; her coming of age as a Jewish girl in an anti-Semitic regime; her early loves and her student days; her encounters with the KGB as an English interpreter in the 1960s and again in the 1980s as the wife of human rights activist Boris Altschuler.

Miller's striking personality shines through her narrative. She radiates kindness and wisdom, seemingly fragile and vulnerable she is able to resist all ideological influences, remaining completely independent-minded and vibrantly alive.

Glas New Russian Writing

contemporary Russian literature in English translation

VOLUME 25

Back issues of Glas:

Larissa Miller

Dim and Distant Days

Translated by Kathleen Cook & Natalie Roy

glas

Editors:

Natasha Perova & Arch Tait & Joanne Turnbull

Front cover: a drawing by Elena Kolat
Camera-ready copy: Tatiana Shaposhnikova

GLAS Publishers (Russia)
Moscow 119517, P.O.Box 47, Russia
tel./tax: +7(095)441 9157
e-mail: perova@glas.msk.su

GLAS Publishers (UK)
Dept. of Russian Literature,
University of Birmingham, Birmingham, B15 2TT, UK
tel/fax: +44(0)121-414 6047
e-mail: a.l.tait@bham.ac.uk

UK and EUROPE
Central Books Ltd., 99 Wallis Road, London E9 5LN, UK
tel: 181-986 4854; fax: 181-533 5821
e-mail: orders@centralbooks.com

USA and Canada
Ivan R. Dee
1332 North Halsted St., Chicago, Illinois 60622-2694, USA
tel: 1-312-787 6262; fax: 1-312-787 6269
toll-free: +1-800-462-6420
e-mail: elephant@ivanrdee.com

WORLD WIDE WEB:
www.russianpress.com/glas
www.bham.ac.uk/glas

ISBN 5-7172-0051-X

Printed at the 'Novosti' printing press, Moscow

CONTENTS

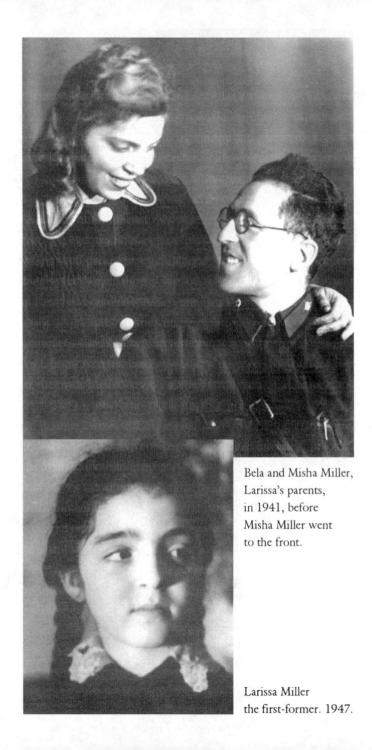

Bela and Misha Miller,
Larissa's parents,
in 1941, before
Misha Miller went
to the front.

Larissa Miller
the first-former. 1947.

Bela Miller, correspondent of the *Red Army Men*. 1942.

Larissa's Grandfather, Granny and Mother. 1957.

Larissa at sixteen.

Larissa at 26.

LEFT:
Larissa in summer
camp. 1951.

Larissa and her mother
at the Black Sea. 1954.

Boris Altschuler, Larissa's husband, a human-rights activist, in the early 1980s.

Larissa in the early 1980s.

I write my memoirs. Labouring
Over dim and distant days
And feel I never shall return
From the past's embracing maze.

With the shadows close around me
I speak silently and smile,
Shed tears. And refuse to talk
The jargon of the present day.

Homo Ludens

In lieu of an Introduction

However complex the world we live in, the hardest thing of all is keeping order in the territory entrusted to us, our own heart and mind, and dealing with the conflicts that arise constantly on the invisible boundary between our space and the space outside. Nothing could be easier, one might think, than to go back and forth as the fancy takes you. But no. Someone is watching the boundary. And that someone is you. You either block all the ways in and feed on external impressions or you obstruct the exits, withdrawing into yourself. You open up your heart to destroy or squander your treasures. There is no peace, no order, no harmony in us. There used to be, of course, but that was long ago, in childhood, when everything was crystal clear, all boundaries.

This inner territory lives a mysterious life of its own, in its own epoch, with its own time count that rarely coincides with the one outside. Inside there is quiet, outside there is uproar; inside all prospers, outside all collapses. Or the reverse: outside is the Renaissance, inside the Dark Middle Ages; outside the snow is melting, inside, the frost nips hard; the outside world is on the verge of new life, but your inner clock has almost stopped. You thought it would go on forever, but that proved to be just one of the illusions in which life abounds. Illusions are a substitute

DIM AND DISTANT DAYS / 15

for happiness, and milestones on our life's path. Moving from one milestone to the next, or rather, from one mirage to the next, we eventually arrive at a new mirage. Not a new one, but an old one that has arisen and vanished a million times before in other hearts. We arrive at a point where others have been before us and left endless evidence that both delights (hooray, I'm not the only one!) and depresses us (alas, I'm not the only one!).

Yet all the same our inner territory remains a terra incognita, and on it we are Adam, whom the Lord plays up to, by giving fresh paints and vivid sensations. 'My first snow,' we exclaim, entranced. 'First lark. First love.'

You think your inner space is endless but suddenly discover that you've tramped the full length and breadth of it, exhausted all its resources, looked into all its recesses. And now there is nothing left, nor is there likely to be anything new. Even commodity exchange between the two worlds, outer and inner, is now impossible.

God endowed you with a divine spark capable of transforming banality into revelation, an ordinary shrub into a 'burning bush'. He gave you inspiration, but you... Yet the Lord giveth and the Lord taketh away. Who knows the whys and wherefores? No matter what theories we may concoct, they all boil down to a nursery rhyme that goes something like this: 'There once lived a little hog, or was it a little dog, perhaps a piglet, maybe a twiglet, or probably no one lived...'

Childhood
in Post-War Moscow

When one is a child, anything can serve as a foothold: Granny's faded apron which she wears constantly (even in bed?); the orange lampshade with its long soiled fringe; the doorbell, which you can barely reach on the third jump. All these little things create stability.

My native land is Bolshaya Polyanka Street. I will never forget this point of reference in space: 10 Bolshaya Polyanka, Apt. 2. My native land is the church domes, the Udarnik cinema, the Moskva River, the neighbouring Ordynka and Yakimanka streets. That's where our local fool lived. He was nicknamed 'Pear'. He had an oblong head and a strange manner of squatting every few steps. He would hurry along, jump up and down, then suddenly squat and gaze around with a happy grin. Thus he reached the food store. The post-war store presented a sorry sight: crutches, amputated limbs, hoarse voices, crying children. And Pear squatting serenely by the counter. No one said a rude word to him, much less chased him away. Our local store catered to war invalids, but I thought the store was called 'invalid' after the one-armed sculptures of a boy and a girl flanking the counter. Each carried on his remaining arm a basket of fruit. And each admired, head tilted back, what the missing hand once held. I didn't mind the dreary bread line and the stuffiness: I was enchanted by the two gypsum figures.

It seemed incredible that they, so smart-looking, should be cripples like those who were queuing for rations on their crutches and stumps. Oddly enough, I pitied not the live cripples, who peopled my world then, but the tasteless dolls. I comforted myself by mentally restoring the missing limbs and putting in their hands all sorts of things: a bunch of grapes, an apple, a bag of my favourite candy. I loved to suck a candy as I strolled through the backyards to my grey four-story block of flats. There it was: two windows on the ground floor, and a boiler room in the basement. Every time I entered our communal apartment, our untidy fat neighbour would appear before me with a towel around her head: 'Lara, for God's sake, don't slam the door. You're a Young Pioneer, aren't you? I have a migraine,' she would whine.

Her consumptive husband was as thin as a rail. With his sunken eyes, dark circles, and violet cheeks, he seemed to have no face; only a profile. I would fall asleep and wake up to his shuffling, coughing and groaning. In some mysterious way, I was identified with him because I was regularly taken to the clinic for a TB test and I was known as a 'bacilli-carrier'.

Their handicapped 30-year-old daughter Vera had a soft spot for me. On hearing my steps, she would call me, loudly and imperatively. This cripple with white baby-like limbs and a wandering smile was confined to her wheel-chair. Trying to concentrate her drifting gaze on me, she would ask, lisping and showering me with saliva: 'Well, my dear, how are you doing at school? All right? I mean, really all right? That's a girl!' Vera smelled of milk, like a baby, and of mustiness, like old rags.

Moronic Vera, her consumptive father, the grubby toilet, the fly-blown lamp in the kitchen — if any of these had disappeared, it would have left a gaping void. Any absurdity, any ugliness that has existed from earliest memories, becomes a foothold of stability in a child's world.

A couple of weeks before Christmas, Granny and I would start making decorations for the tree. Granny made glue, pulled out rolls of coloured paper and two pairs of scissors, and we would set to work. I was too slow and clumsy, so Granny, losing patience, would take the scissors and glue out of my hands, and finish the job. She would leave only simple tasks for me, like arranging the finished toys in a box and throwing out the scraps. But even that gave me pleasure. The only thing that made my heart sink was fear that Granny would get angry at me for being so awkward. Her wrath was always tempestuous, she would scream and throw things — anything that happened to be around. 'You Nazi brat!' she growled, her lips trembling. 'Why, you Nazi brat!' She would fly off the handle if I left something uneaten on my plate or failed to do a maths problem. But whenever the evening passed peacefully, I was happy.

In the process of making toys for the Christmas tree, she would forget all about time. The clock hissed, then chimed 9 o'clock. Then 10. My eyelids would close under their own weight. Grandfather dozed on the couch, his face covered with a newspaper which rose and fell with his breathing. I wished the evening would go on forever but what lay ahead was also good. New Year's Eve was a special, mysterious and happy event. Mother and Granny would 'revive' my last year's costume: sew some new cotton wool onto the crown, paste new spangles on mother's old velvet dressing gown, and I became the Snow-Maiden again. I would be performing an improvised dance around the Christmas tree when, with a sudden loud knock on the door, Grandfather Frost would appear in his long gown with a cotton wool hat and collar camouflaging his face. 'Sholom Aleichem, my dears, and Happy New Year,' he would say. Grandfather's exaggeratedly loud voice and his transformed appearance made me freeze in anticipation of miracles.

There were other festive occasions which Mother would arrange for the two of us. In the middle of a week of working almost round the clock, she would suddenly be given a day off. For me it meant playing hooky, because on such days Mother let me stay home from school. We would start planning the day before. The next day dawned. In the morning, through my sleep, I heard the door lock click. That meant Mother had left for the local market. On such holidays Mother would get up early, pull on her dress right over her nightie, put her coat on top of all this and hurry off. She always returned with something special, depending on the season: a jar of baked cream with a brown skin, a bunch of crimson radishes, a bouquet of lilac or mimosa. We would sort through her bags and packages, look for a vase for the flowers, and wash the vegetables. I liked to wash radishes: it was a pleasure to roll them between my fingers under the stream of water, watching them turn bright red. We had a bowl of fresh greens for breakfast. A bunch of fresh flowers sat on the piano. And that was only the beginning of the day. Breakfast was followed by joyful, hurried preparations. We would go to a matinee at the cinema or the theatre. Mother liked to live it up: if it was the cinema, it had to be a double-feature. If it was the theatre, it would be followed by a cinema or we would have guests afterwards. There would be a lot of activity. We constantly had visitors. In the summer they came right through our ground-floor window. The room was filled with smoke. Ashtrays littered the floor, somebody casually played a gypsy dance on the piano while Mother, red-haired, in her light, flowery frock, would glide around the room, arms spread out, shimmying her shoulders. Sometimes she bent down to some of those sitting and, looking into their eyes, tapped out a dance. Laughter, joking, kisses.

Granny's parties were quite different. She would invite all our relatives. Some of them I saw only at such family gatherings. I don't remember their names or even their voices anymore; I only remember how they used to hold a fork or gnaw on a bone. Granny would get ready for such festive occasions with inspiration and gusto. At the set hour, gefilte fish would appear on the table, red horseradish sauce in separate saucers, and a bowl of 'pigeons' (rissoles rolled in cabbage-leaves) tied with thread. That thread gave me no peace. 'What's it for?' I would ask every time. 'To tie the pigeons' wings so they don't fly away,' I was told. I would suck the salty thread for a long time, then put it away in my pocket.

We were visited regularly by a tall, burly man who looked like a gypsy with a bushy moustache and a gold tooth. He wore a capacious coat and a broad-brimmed hat and comported himself with dignity. 'Our court cobbler' we used to call him. The gypsy would squat down, legs wide apart, place his travelling bag that smelt of leather, glue and polish between them, then with a flourish take out our old shoes, now miraculously transformed and shining. They could have been crystal slippers, so carefully and lovingly did he put them down in front of us.

Our magic cobbler would often bring his own wares, the creations of his own hands. I was not a spoilt child, but one day he put out a pair of brown slippers with little bows and very elegant heels. Remembering that modesty was my main virtue (greatly valued by Granny), I said nothing, but could not take my eyes off them. In the end the cobbler made me a smaller identical pair, which I cherished rather than wore. I used to put them next to me when I did my homework and on a chair by my bed when I slept. As soon as I grew out of them a new pair appeared, an exact copy of the first. I wore out my last pair in 1956. The 'court cobbler' was a magician. He even produced his handkerchief like a conjurer, pulling away endlessly out of his pocket. How could he have wiped that dark-skinned bald patch and huge forehead with an ordinary-sized one?

Another cobbler lived across the street on the ground floor of a low sturdy house. He sat by the window (wide open in summer) in his big leather apron, muttering under his breath and tapping away with his hammer, making holes with his awl, gluing something or patching felt boots. And we, children, stood by the window and watched. 'Only don't get in my light,' he used to say. The whole street went to him. 'Help us out, Petrovich.' And he did.

Not far away lived Mother's dressmaker Nina Iosifovna: first floor, back entrance. Her windows faced the side wall of the neighbouring block, so she had to have the light on all day (probably as a penalty for living in her own, albeit minute, flat instead of in a communal flat like most people). Everything there was fascinating: the foot-pedal sewing machine, the bobbins, pins and different coloured scraps of cloth that I was allowed to collect, and the glossy fashion magazines. It was interesting to watch her, kneeling in front of Mother with her mouth full of pins, as she created something that rustled and shone on Mother, then surveyed her creation, squinting, in the long mirror that hung in the corridor.

A special attraction in the flat was her husband, Nikolai Ivanovich. When we arrived, he would say hello and hurry off to his well-lit corner to work, copying out music. He had plenty of orders and was always busy, but did everything with great care and on time. I used to peep over his shoulder and watch the black and white strings of notes, sharps and flats, heads and tails appear with magical speed.

Nina Iosifovna only made very special things — dress suits and evening gowns, and only of expensive fabrics, so Mother did not go to her very often, but wore what she made for a long time.

If we needed something light, cheap and summery we would invite Zheshka. She must have been about sixty, but everyone called her by her first name. Getting Zheshka to make something meant having her to stay. She had nothing of her own, no family, children or place to live, so she was always staying with people, but she never complained about her lot. Quite the opposite, she regarded herself as the fortunate possessor of a happy disposition, excellent taste and, most important, a perfect figure. Crossing her slim legs and unstitching Mother's old housecoat, she would recount the by now familiar stories about her brief career as a ballerina in the corps de ballet, about the lovelorn sculptor who once sculpted her legs in the dim and distant past, and about a new friend, 'a good-looker who simply slays the men'. But her favourite was the one about an admirer who followed her along the street until he caught her up and saw her face. One look and he fled. At this point Zheshka would roar with laughter. She was really ugly, but made fun even of that.

A week later, somewhat dazed by Zheshka's incessant chatter, we were gazing admiringly at Mother's new outfit in the mirror. Light and airy, one might even say, smart. No one would ever have thought it was made from an old dress.

Over the Stone Bridge by the Udarnik cinema was our hairdressing salon where Mother often took me with her for company and for fun. I used to entertain those present by reciting poems and singing songs. Vertinsky's songs were most popular, and I always had to give an encore. The hairdressers were like lords, aloof and punctilious, they used to kiss their lady's hand. One of them, grey-haired and dignified, was, of course, the supreme lord and master artist. All of them, irrespective of their size, fluttered around their ladies in their spotlessly white coats, like butterflies round a flower, using their tongs with nonchalant skill: warming them, cooling them, flourishing them in the air and putting them to their lips to ensure they were the right temperature to create something fancy on their lady's head. The huge mirrors, spacious halls and large windows — which for some reason had marble busts of Roman goddesses, or was it matrons, cracked with age on their sills — made it look more like a palace than a hairdresser's.

Our own hairdresser, our own cobbler and our own dressmaker... Yet Mother and I could hardly survive from one pay-day to the next, particularly when there were just the two of us. But each time we did survive, we had a feast: we bought two pastries in Stoleshnikov Lane (the Stoleshnikov pastry shop was famous) and a hundred grams of good cheese at the cheese shop in Gorky Street. The smell of cheese in that shop was so delicious! The assistants and even the sign outside seemed to be made of butter and fresh cream.

In fact the Moscow of the late forties and fifties was a million temptations, a town created for Mother and me to enjoy. Take the Hermitage Gardens. We sometimes spent the whole of Sunday there, walking, reading, dreaming on a bench, and going to see the Raikin comic show in the evening. The dense foliage gave the gardens an air of mystery, but the shady paths always led to a small cafe or kiosk. In the daytime the park was quiet and fairly deserted, but in the evening the different coloured lights lit up, well-dressed people appeared on the paths and a brass band played on the bandstand. The Summer and Winter theatres both had something to offer and there were films at the cinema, so you didn't know where to go first.

Not far from the Hermitage in one of the side streets lived a furrier whom I had been longing to visit ever since I first heard this strange word from Mother. To my disappointment the furrier turned out to be an ordinary elderly woman, whose only distinctive feature was a blue spot on her lip. Even that was not particularly interesting. 'It was an accident with a pin,' Mother told me. Her apartment exceeded all my expectations, however. It was a real den, where furs and pelts lived a still, dark life of their own. They lay in piles on the wide divan, stretched out prostrate on the table or hung pinned together on a wooden female dummy that revolved on one leg. But the real lair was the huge mirrored wardrobe with black, brown and silver furs lying on its numerous shelves, and fur coats and other articles of fur hanging on special frames. Just pull them aside and you could step into a dense forest from which there was no return. Many years later, reading C. S. Lewis's *The Lion, the Witch and the Wardrobe* to my children, I remembered this deep mysterious wardrobe. 'But what could Mother have been doing at a furrier's?' I wondered just now. Then I suddenly remembered her coat with the astrakhan collar and hat — Mother's one and only winter outfit for many years.

'Tsar, tsarevich, king, prince, cobbler, tailor, who are you?' we used to chant in my childhood that was spent in post-war Moscow, a chaotic but surprisingly cosy city, because of ordinary people living their everyday lives. I was too small to appreciate their work, but in their very behaviour, which was leisurely and artistic, in their fine, confident movements, you could sense dignity, substance, integrity, a feeling of belonging. Even Zheshka, who seemed to live as she sewed — come what may — had her own style, her own magical touch.

Then there was the clockmaker I had heard about but never seen. Grandfather had been taking all our broken watches and clocks to him since before the war. There was also Doctor Belenky, the children's doctor. Mother said he knew everything about his tiny patients and even let them tinkle on him and twist his nose. In spite of his impressive size he had very gentle, sensitive hands that tapped and tickled almost all of new-born Moscow.

King, prince, cobbler, tailor... And each of them really was a king in his own tiny kingdom, living by the laws of honour. Each of them was a holdover of the 'accursed past', a relic who had miraculously preserved his or her noble qualities despite countless actions by the state designed to obliterate the individual.

Today these people are almost extinct, and without them even the most densely populated world seems empty. No, I don't want to pull the present day to pieces — a tedious and pointless occupation. It's just that living in a desert and feeling a natural thirst, I try to quench it the only way I can, by kneeling down at the old, long exhausted springs. Maybe they can still refresh, who knows.

* * *

Sometimes my childhood world began to list. Once somebody rushed into our yard, shouting: 'A boy's got under a tram!' We all rushed out into the street. Even I went with them, breaking my solemn promise never to leave the yard. A little boy lay on the tracks. He lay still. Only his right hand twitched slightly. I couldn't tear my eyes away from that hand, sun-tanned, covered with red spots. A wooden outbuilding stood across the road. Sitting on the windowsill on the second floor was the boy's mother, swaying and wailing. It seemed strange that she didn't run down to the tracks. She was wrapped in something large and black as she swayed and wailed. Her wailing and that twitching hand gave me no sleep that night and haunted me for a long time afterwards.

As a child, I thought death was brown. Because the little boy's hand was brown from the sun. And the neighbour's boy who drowned in the river was also dark. He had tanned during the summer, and lay all brown in his coffin. Also brown and wrinkled was the face of the old lady doctor who died during the war. Granny and I walked behind the horse-drawn cart with the casket as it bumped along the cobbled street. That was my first memory of death. Granny told me the doctor had cured me when I was dying from dyspepsia. She had got apples somewhere for me, a rarity in those days. I don't remember ever seeing the doctor alive, but I clearly remember her lying in the coffin: her wrinkled swarthy face, and the snow-white lace cap on her head. Because of the apples, which Granny mentioned so many times, the doctor's face seemed like a baked apple to me.

My image of death as something brown was later destroyed when the woman upstairs committed suicide. I had often met that proud tall woman with a fancy felt hat on her head. Her husband, a short fat Jew, was always in a hurry, but whenever he passed me he would crack a joke and invite me to their place. They said he was an army surgeon. He always wore an army uniform, which did not become his short fat figure. One day he disappeared. I heard mother whisper to someone that he had been 'put away.' I had thought that only bandits and thieves were jailed, and hard as I tried I couldn't associate that word with him.

One day people in our house started rushing about, bewailing someone, there was great commotion. That was when I first heard the expression 'committed suicide.' The surgeon's wife had committed suicide. That death was remote, unseen. Death hovered somewhere upstairs, on the top floor, where we never went. Death had visited that tall, proud, enigmatic woman. She hadn't drowned, she hadn't got under a tram, she hadn't grown old, she hadn't fallen ill. She had taken her life. Those were strange, incomprehensible, hermetic words, like the heavy drapes on the windows of the apartment where the ruined family lived. On the day of the funeral, we children stood downstairs, looking up at the curtained windows. It seemed to me that every now and then a pale flickering light shimmered behind the drapes, as if a candle was being carried around.

Thereafter death ceased to be something tangible and lost its colour. I knew that people died, but that happened somewhere on another floor, in the next house, outside the gate. I didn't know then that one's family could also die — those who determined my life. That experience would come later, but would not teach me anything. I never felt any better and never became accustomed to it just because it happened again and again. As the years went by, my understanding of death broadened: death was no longer simply breathing one's last. Death was any loss, any disintegration, anything irreversible, which was hard to believe. Yet once in a while my childhood faith that everything in this world could be remedied and reversed returned, the faith that wholeness could be restored. As if the elements of the whole keep forever the memory of the former unity and are ready to reunite given a happy coincidence. But where is that happy coincidence? Your whole life could pass without such a coincidence. To make sure that things were remediable, you'd have to live forever. Only in childhood is everything easily reparable. So great is the urge to live and the joy of living, and so numerous the reasons for it, they don't have to be sought.

A day in April. Or was it April? In any case, it was Easter. I remember the sky, bottomless and fluid. It seemed there was no sky at all, only a quivering blueness and weightlessness. Wherever you set your foot, there were springs and streams of clear water. On such a day, stagnation in nature or in life or in thoughts seemed impossible. Everything was fluid.

But I couldn't understand any of that then. I only remember the sky and the flowing water. I remember it was chilly and I was trying to stick my hands into the shallow pockets of my new beige overcoat. Actually, it wasn't new: it had been altered from Mother's old coat but it was the first time I had put it on. 'Overcoat turned inside out' — I had heard these words so often at the end of the winter that I associated them with the anticipation of spring, the melting snow, the thaws, my eyes smarting from the brightness and blueness of everything. The original colour of Mother's old coat, turned inside out, looked especially bright against the background of the right side. The inner side, which had retained its original colour, became the outside. The original colour always showed: even if the coat was not turned inside out, then the sleeves were let out, or the hem was lengthened. Strips of the original colour showed everywhere. And they meant spring.

Why I remember that particular day in April, I don't know. Nothing unusual happened on that Easter Sunday. I stood in the yard next to the wooden table which smelled of wet paint, watching the old women file through the yard. They went in groups or alone, some with their grandchildren. Each carried a neat bundle, some had paper flowers. These old women seemed to be an organic part of the flowing azure day. In the middle of the yard stood a group of Young Pioneers their scratch-pads poised. They promptly and cheerfully took down the names of the children whom they caught going to church, so as to denounce them to their teacher. That was their Young Pioneer assignment for Easter.

May Day was not too far off. Wheat flour would soon be available for coupons. And again huge lines would crawl along the street, like a many-eyed, many-armed, many-legged monster. Then we children would be in great demand. We would skip school and be rented out by adults to get an extra ration of flour. We would show each other our hands with the violet ink numbers indicating our place in line and argue whose number was higher. The blue ink number on my palm, the human line droning like a beehive, my overcoat with flour all over it, missing classes, the spring — that was real happiness.

When the boiler-room door wasn't padlocked that meant the stoker, Uncle Peter, was inside. We would hurry down the steep, dim staircase to watch Uncle Peter throwing coal into the stove, lazily swearing under his breath. In the spring, similarly swearing under his breath, he would trim the lilacs in the garden, because he was also a gardener. My Granny had planted those lilac bushes in her younger days. Mother had told me that many times. Uncle Peter would go with his stepladder from bush to bush while we children bustled about, gathering the cut branches. The air smelled of freshly clipped lilac and Uncle Peter's cheap tobacco.

In the evening, Granny and I would go to the trolley-bus stop to meet Mother. She usually left for the radio studio at dawn and returned late in the evening. That's how people worked in those days. One trolley-bus would go by, another, a third. There she was at last. We were never quite sure we would see her, so when she did appear we were overjoyed. At night Mother typed up her endless 'Mailbags' to be broadcast the next day to Scandinavia. That was the name of a program in which a Soviet journalist condescendingly informed naive foreign listeners about the advantages of Soviet life.

The tapping of the typewriter was the night sound of my childhood. From time to time the typing would stop: Mother would get up to smoke and think. Cigarette smoke was the night smell of my childhood. Toward morning, Mother would lie down next to me. But by the time I woke, she would be gone. She would leave an unfinished cup of tea and a cigarette butt with pink lipstick on it.

The sweetest time was just before I fell asleep, when I lived in my fantasy world, where everything ended the way I wanted. I would pull my left hand from under the blanket and hold it near the floor until it got cold. The cold hand was some unfortunate lost in the woods. My right hand (under the blanket) was myself. This hand groped under the pillow and in the folds of the blanket. That was me roaming the woods in search of the lost one. And finally — O joy — one hand would find the other. The lost one would be rescued. I'd put him under the blanket: get warm now!

Once, during such fantasising, I heard Mother's voice: 'Evgeny, come on over.' That was how Evgeny appeared in our life. Someone tall, gaunt, bespectacled, with a pale pimply face and straight greasy hair stood between me and Mother. Every now and then he would shake his head to get the hair out of his eyes. Mother said he was a philosopher. I didn't know what a philosopher was and for a long time associated the word with his paleness, pimples and glasses. Evgeny would sometimes tell me about a fiery chariot and make egg-flip. In fact, he seldom made it: either we didn't have eggs or we didn't have sugar. But when we had both, he beat the egg-yolk with such zeal that sweat streamed from his brow and his hair stuck to it. My fear that his sweat would drip into the cup spoiled the whole treat.

Late in the evening, Mother and Evgeny would have visitors. Evgeny played something of his own composition on the piano. More precisely, the music was his, the lyrics were Mother's. She sang while he hammered away, slightly jumping and sticking out his thumbs: 'You took away my heart in the old mail-van,' or something of the sort.

Once I was awoken by Evgeny's nasty hissing: 'Go back to bed! Off with you!' I woke up to find myself standing at Mother's bedside, barefoot, in my nightie. I was scared: how on earth had I got there from the other room? After a few nights, I realised I was sleep-walking. It had started with Evgeny's appearance in our life: I must have become jealous when I was moved to the other room. Characteristically, my sleep-walking ceased when Evgeny disappeared. We were rather poor, and when Mother caught Evgeny pilfering sugar from the cupboard — the precious sugar she had put aside for me — she kicked him out. I don't know if that was the real reason or not, but in any case Evgeny disappeared. The world returned to normal.

'Only please don't ask questions until the end of the film,' mother begged me each time. 'I'll explain everything to you afterwards.' I would keep quiet for about ten minutes, then start tugging at her sleeve and whispering: 'Are they Russians or

Germans? Is that our lot or their lot? Who are the baddies?' One day when a man with a moustache and a pince-nez appeared on the screen I whispered loudly: 'Is he a baddy? Mum, is he a baddy?' Mother looked round anxiously, grabbed me roughly by the arm and hissed: 'Be quiet!' Her fury was so unexpected and so inexplicable that I immediately lost all interest in the film and sat there, sniffling and rubbing away the tears that were trickling down my cheeks. Mother went on looking straight ahead and made no attempt to comfort me. Only when we got home did she explain that the man I had taken for a baddy was none other than Molotov, our foreign minister, and that she could have got into real trouble. 'I forbid you to ask me questions in the cinema. Is that clear?' It was.

Finding myself alone with the screen, I felt a bit taken aback at first, but then decided to try and work things out for myself. To this day I remember my first independent conclusion. I can't be sure what the film was called, but the scene was of some very important-looking bigwigs in a large study. One of them I recognised straightaway — it was Stalin, whose appearance on the screen was always greeted by tumultuous applause. The rest were all people I did not know. One corpulent man went up to the fireplace and stood there with his back to the open grate then, suddenly feeling the heat, he either jumped away quickly. That made the audience laugh. 'He must be bad,' I decided happily. I could hardly wait until the film was over to share my discovery with Mother and she confirmed it. The fat man's name was Churchill and although he wasn't a German, he wasn't one of us either. A new stage had begun in my career as a cinema-goer — the stage of independent conclusions.

No sooner had I embarked on this path, however, than life put a spanner in the works. Foreign films, usually war trophies, were not often shown in those days. People flocked to see them. We went as well, and to a very late show. Children were not allowed, of course, so Mother smuggled me in under her coat. Everything about this film was strange — the title: *Scandal in Clochemerle*, which meant nothing to me, the late hour, and my smuggled-in presence. The picture was not shown in the regular hall at our local cinema, the Udarnik, but in the small hall on the ground floor. When the lights went down, something I was quite unprepared for began. All sorts of people with funny names began rushing about, gesticulating and making a fuss on the screen. I tried tugging at my mother's sleeve, but she was laughing so hard she didn't even notice. The audience was roaring but I could not join in however hard I tried. Feeling miserable and rejected, I decided to watch my mother's face, in the hope of laughing at the right moment. The only thing I knew for certain was that when the film was over I wouldn't have the slightest idea what to ask. My usual questions were no good. On the way home I asked the only possible one: 'What was the film about?' 'The opening of a public lavatory,' I was told. I shrugged my shoulders in bewilderment.

No, it was better to go to our films where I had learnt to sort things out a bit. One day I got so cocky I even tried expressing my own critical judgement and in reply to Granny's question about what I thought of a new film I said casually: 'Not bad'. 'Well, I never!' she exclaimed. 'People worked hard, wasted their time and effort, so that you could turn up your nose at them like a snooty little bourgeois miss!' This reaction checked my desire to be critical. Mother also preferred to praise everything she saw. She followed this principle all her life, buying several season tickets to each international film festival and seeing everything regardless. In reply to my bewildered questions she would say: 'You must learn to discover something good in everything. Even in a bad picture you can find something interesting if you try: see how people live, how they dress and what they do in their spare time. Going to the cinema is like visiting another country.'

In those very early days many years ago Moscow was echoing with the unforgettable name of Tarzan. This film was as simple and clear as the dialogue between the two main characters 'Jane — Tarzan. Tarzan — Jane'. I even managed through my own observations to conclude that there was no point in getting all worked up when the hero or heroine was teetering on the brink of a precipice, because the only ones to go over the edge would be the slaves and the blacks.

One film in my childhood left me absolutely spellbound: *The Indian Tomb*. The enigmatic beauty of the characters, their strange movements, exotic dances, sumptuous palaces and white elephants were so unusual that my questions dried up completely. Particularly as it was only Mother whom I pestered with my many question, whereas I went to see *The Indian Tomb* with Granny and Grandfather. Coming out afterwards, we walked home slowly through snow-covered Moscow with me singing the theme song from the film and Grandfather whistling it, a song I remember to this day.

There is one film with which I have a special, complicated and very personal relationship: *The First-Former*. When I first saw this film (and I saw it a great many times) and came home excited and full of impressions, they told me something that really took my breath away. Apparently the children's writer Agnia Barto, whom Mother and I often visited, had advised the makers of the film to invite me to play the main role. One of the film crew came to discuss terms, but Granny was categorically against the idea. 'No, I won't let them cripple the child! I won't allow them to ruin her life!' Cripple, ruin, I couldn't get these two words out of my head. Each time I saw *The First-Former* I relived the tragedy over again. I had been crippled, my life had been ruined. Although I have forgotten the film almost completely, I still remember the face of the girl who played the part instead of me. Her name was Natasha Zaschipina. Sitting in the dark cinema, I invariably experienced the 'Frog Princess' syndrome and could hardly keep from telling everyone: 'That's me. I should have acted in this film. That's my part!'

No, I was not destined to be an actress. I remained a spectator, but a sensitive, loyal, grateful and responsive one. And that's not a bad role either.

My first close friend was Galia Zaitseva, tow-headed and snub-nosed. She lived in the apartment next door. We communicated by tapping on the wall and we would frequently drop in on each other. One day she and I decided to stage Marshak's play *The Twelve Months* for the New Year's Eve. We distributed the parts among the neighbourhood children. I was to be the stage director since the idea was mine, and so was the book. Each picked the part he liked best. I wanted very much to be the poor but virtuous Step Daughter who looked for snowdrops in the forest, but I magnanimously gave the part to Galia. I was the stage director, after all, and it was unbecoming to grab the best role too. I would be the Princess, wilful and eccentric. Late in the evening, as I sat at the table copying the lines for the other actors, the doorbell rang. 'Where's your Lara?' The door of our room opened and Galia's mother burst in, followed by Granny.

'Who do you think you are?' she railed. 'How dare you make my girl the Step-Daughter? You think you can be a Princess and she's going to be a Step-Daughter, eh? You have no right! I know you Kikes. Always out for number one.' She turned to Granny: 'And where've you been, Madam? You think you can teach the teachers while your granddaughter is making fun of my child? She'll never come here again! Princess, my foot!' Granny tried to say something, but Galia's mother wouldn't listen and rushed out.

The play was off. But that didn't spoil our friendship. I would signal to Galia, as before, when I was going out, and she would tap back or call out the window: 'Coming! I'm getting dressed.'

The older I got, the harder it was to find consolation and the fewer were the events and chores I could bury my cares in. The early morning hours were not so sweet as before. And the events of the day were disturbing.

'Go away! You're a Jew!' the oldest of my friends declared.

'What does that mean?' I asked.

'Jews have black hair. Jews are bad. Remember how you pushed me when I had a sore foot?'

I didn't remember, but my brain started feverishly putting two and two together: Jew, black hair, pushed. I had to go home and ask. 'Don't listen to her,' Granny said. 'She's just a silly girl.'

But how could I not listen when a whole gang now followed me around the yard, chanting:

> *What's the time, kids?*
> *My watch says: three Yids*
> *And a dirty kike,*
> *All riding a bike!*

That's when I realised I was totally defenceless. It seemed to me that if I'd had a father, even a sick old man, always coughing like our neighbour, everything would have been different. But what could Mother, Granny and my meek grandfather do against a gang of kids? After all, my family was just as vulnerable.

For the first time I felt I was different. Did I imagine then that henceforth I would be an outcast and that there was no escape? No, I had no idea. At the time, I was sure I would go into the yard the next morning and see the other children's repentant faces. Luda Vedemina, the oldest of the girls, would come up to me and say... I couldn't imagine what exactly she would say, but my heart would miss a beat and my eyes would brim.

However the next morning, the teasing started again and I felt the ground slipping from under my feet. The ground slipping away — sometimes it's a sweet feeling. Once a boy I had been playing with in the yard said he was thirsty and wanted to go home. He invited me to come along. That was the first time I found myself inside a house I'd seen only from the outside. From the yard, the house was familiar down to the last little scratch on the wall, but suddenly I found myself in a strange room. One moment had separated the usual from the unusual, the street din from the quiet, the sunshine from the indoor dusk. The usual was revealed to me from a new point of view. Everything started to swim before my eyes: the lacy curtains, the ticking alarm clock, the carafe on the table.

I had once experienced the same dizziness in the country, when I got lost and found myself in a dank gully, blue with forget-me-nots. I gathered them, kneeling in the damp moss, oblivious to everything. When I remembered where I was, I was scared I wouldn't find my way back, and ran out of the gully. A few moments later I saw the familiar roof and realised I was near home. From this new vantage point, our house looked strange, unreal.

When such things happen, the trite, boring connections disappear. Everything breaks up. It is not destroyed, but disintegrates into self-contained moments which can later be reconnected, but in a different, unpredictable order. Meanwhile, you're out of the game, you view everything, even your own life, as if from a distance. Not that you're an outcast — no, you're in full harmony with the world, merged with it, but it has fallen apart into separate moments which have, however, retained their beauty and integrity.

What a strange passion it is — to reminisce! A summer's day. My first day in the summer camp. We children are being put to bed. The camp-beds are lined up outside. The teacher commands, 'Now, go to bed, quick! I'll count to three: one, two...' I climb in under the blanket, placing my head on the regulation pillow with the faded violet stamp 'Kindergarten of the Paris Commune Factory.' I'm homesick. Mother is far away in Moscow. I am surrounded by strangers. It is the loathsome mid-day nap — 'dead hour' — in the bright sunshine. Adults walk around nearby, talking quietly. A new girl has just arrived from the city. She's late, so she is given lunch and allowed not to sleep. She has an incredibly squeaky voice. Her mother is issuing last-minute instructions, calling her 'birdie.' I listen with envy to the birdie's squeak, I watch the tops of the slender trees swaying and creaking in the wind. Gradually another feeling mixes with my homesickness: a feeling of novelty, of the blue sky, of the white birches, the smell of the grass, of the forest, of fresh linen; the dizziness from the clouds drifting overhead, the quivering leaves, the swaying treetops; also the feeling of being an orphan, ·abandoned in this fluid, newly-discovered space, where you are alone with the sky, the trees, the wind; the feeling of being abandoned by everyone. It's remarkable how many words must be used — words I didn't even know at the age of six — that fail, in the end, to convey even a fraction of what I felt then. The summer of 1946 was rich in such discoveries.

A rainy morning. No outings. We children have been seated at a long table on the veranda with pencils and paper. As the rain beats on the window pane, we draw, wheezing and sniffling. Our teacher sits in the corner, sharpening pencils. The shavings' smell of wood, the lead becomes sharp as a needle, and the colourful heap of freshly sharpened pencils grows. I could draw only a few objects: a sun looking like a daisy, a cottage with a triangular roof, a humanoid creature with a braid, trees and mushrooms. Despite this poverty of subject matter, I used up a lot of paper, creating many multicoloured worlds, which only whetted my appetite for more. For a time, drawing became my all-consuming passion. Whenever I could find some paper and a pencil, I drew, wishing to recapture the creative fervour of that rainy morning. But I failed. Perhaps I missed the crowd of fellow-draughtsmen and the rain pattering on the windows. Ever since, I've yearned for that intent silence which gave birth to colourful worlds.

Peering into moments long passed is like poring over old photographs. Here's one: children in shorts and T-shirts sitting on the grass around a woman in a white smock — Kira Ivanovna, our music teacher. She had a wondrous instrument, which she always brought to class and placed beside her on a stool. At the start of the lesson, she hit it with a tiny hammer. It emitted a sound, which she quickly took up. 'Laaa,' Kira Ivanovna sang, gesturing to us to follow. 'Laaa', we squeaked after her. She hit the tuning fork again and repeated more insistently: 'Laaa.' Then squatting in front of each child, she put her ear right up to his lips. 'Laaa,' the timid ones whispered; 'Laaa,' the brave ones shouted. She approached each of us in turn, seeming to draw our very soul out with the sound. Finally, in desperation or satisfaction, she would start the lesson proper.

Once Kira Ivanovna announced that for the Parents Day we were to prepare a concert: songs, dances, and games.

On Parents Day we had two boiled eggs and herring paste for breakfast. Both of which were a real treat after the war. And, most importantly, the overture to this holiday. My pleasure was spoiled only by the fact that my neighbour liked to crack his eggs on my forehead. Which he did so smartly that I never quite managed to dodge him. And since the eggs were not always quite hard-boiled, this could be a problem. Another highlight of the holiday menu was the jam cake for supper. But by then Parents Day was practically over, and however sweet the cake it always stuck in my throat.

Anyway let's begin at the beginning. The beginning was not the morning, but much earlier when the date of Parents Day was first announced. From then onwards I lived in anticipation. Active anticipation, I should say, making presents for Mother. First of all, I tried to find out from the child carers and nannies the words of the songs that they sang in the evening. They were certainly not songs for children, and I knew that Mother liked them but did not know all the words, and how surprised she would be when I sang them from beginning to end. I also dried some flowers and grasses for the herbarium I was planning to give her. Nearer the date I made a wreath, and also picked some wild strawberries and threaded them on a blade of grass.

The night before Parents Day seemed endless. I even got up to use the bucket (which I didn't usually) and in the darkness tripped over a nanny, sleeping on a mattress on the floor. 'Darn and drat yer,' she hissed, pulling the hem of my nightie. I woke up at the crack of dawn, longing to hop out of bed and run to the gate to meet Mother. At last it was time to get up, do our morning exercises and put on one of the standard-issue dresses they gave us for special occasions. What the boys wore, I don't remember. I was too busy with my own attire. How I loved those dresses, slightly starched, with a high collar and frills instead of sleeves, and long since faded flowers on an indeterminate background. The cut and pattern were all the same. They were standard-issue dresses after all. But you could choose your colour... 'Red or lilac?' I couldn't make up my mind. Then one of the boys shouted: 'Red is for fools'. That decided it. I chose the lilac one. It hung like a bell on me, too short and far too wide. But I loved it: the flowers, and the frills, and the fresh smell (they must have hung it up to dry outside). And most important of all, that dress meant Parents Day.

After breakfast the waiting started. Sweet and painful. 'Yours have come!' I could hear on all sides. 'Milka, yours have come!' First I hung around by the fence, jumping up at each 'yours have come'. Then I decided to go off and stop waiting. No sooner had I walked away than I heard the long-awaited 'Larissa, yours have come!' I saw Mother's golden-auburn shock of hair, her shiny earrings and brightly coloured dress. Mother was hunched up as she walked along concealed by bushes. Probably to give me a surprise. But she was too striking to pass unnoticed. 'My little monkey!' She ran up to me, and I hung on her neck. 'Careful or you'll squash everything, the berries and the cake...'

Stay, fleeting moment... And it did. Time stopped and only Mother and I went on. We walked and walked until we came to a clearing in the forest where a hammock from goodness only knows where was hanging. We sat down on it and decided to exchange presents. Out of her bag Mother produced fruit juice, berries, a cake, a box of sugared cranberries, some transfers, a snow-white sun hat with the price tag still on it and a pair of sandals smelling of new leather, which I admired, sniffed and immediately put on. Then she told me to close my eyes tight, took my hand and fastened something round my wrist. What was it? A real watch with a dial and two hands, one pointing at nine and the other at twelve.

I ate the cake, drank the juice, stretched out my legs to see the sandals and moved my arm to admire the watch. What more could one want? But Mother rummaged in her bag again and, lowering her voice, chanted with an enigmatic expression: 'God sent the crow a piece of cheese / The crow perched happily in the trees / To have her breakfast she did think / Then changed her mind, the cheese in her beak...' I stared at Mother eyes wide open, but she went on reciting and took a small book out of her bag: Krylov's *Fables*. Although the paper in the book was grey and thin and there were not many pictures, I fell in love with it straightaway and for many years to come.

Now it was my turn to give her presents. I placed the faded wreath on Mother's head, fed her the squashed strawberries, carefully taking them off the blade of grass, put the herbarium on her lap and studied her face carefully. Was she disappointed? No, she was smiling, that meant she was pleased. Then I sang her the songs, proudly uttering each word, and what I wanted most happened. Mother took out a pencil and paper and wrote the words all down as I dictated.

It was all too good to last forever. Mother looked at her watch and said it was time to go back. I looked at mine and said it couldn't be because the hands hadn't moved. 'But I must go,' she insisted. 'Mustn't break the rules. Otherwise they won't let you off for a whole day again. We set off back. There was the familiar field, the green fence, and our gate with lots of women going through it already, mothers and grandmothers. Hardly any men. They were rare in those post-war years. I held on to Mother, and she had to free her hand gently, but firmly.

So that was it. Now she would go away, and I would wave to her until she disappeared from view. I knew she was crying, afraid to turn round. But then she did, putting both hands to her mouth to blow me a kiss.

'Supper's ready,' someone shouted. Gobbling down his jam pie, my shaven neighbour asked: 'What did you get?' I stretched out a leg to show my sandal-clad foot. 'Pooh. Mine's better.' He pulled out a black pistol with a set of bullets tipped with rubber suckers. 'Want one in the forehead?'

It was getting chilly. Everyone drifted onto the veranda. I could have gone too and done my transfers, but I didn't feel like it. I just wanted to hide in the farthest corner and listen to the trains as they whistled past. Then at nine it would be bedtime.

'Now let's learn a new game: The Heron and the Frogs... Show me how frogs jump in the swamp...All right, good. Now the heron. Now, Frogs, go and hide. Valia, you'll be the Heron.' Valia Baranova, petite, long-legged, started moving, spreading out her arms and raising her knees high. 'All right. Pull your toes in. Good for you. So you be the Heron. You'll wear a starched skirt like a ballet dancer. Who knows what a ballet skirt is called?' 'A tutu,' Valia promptly answered. She took ballet classes, and knew all about it. I eyed her with envy, enraptured. How I would have loved to be in her place. I'd always dreamed of becoming a ballet dancer and badgered Mother to send me to ballet school. Mother did take me somewhere and showed me to someone. I remember a middle-aged man tapping me on the knees and saying: 'What an emaciated creature! She could use some feeding first, Madame. Try bringing her next year.' But next year Mother enrolled me at the neighbouring music school, evidently deciding that was enough. And now this concert, the Heron, the tutu. I could think of nothing else. I would run off to a secret place and rehearse: strut around, spreading out my arms, lifting my knees high, stretching out my toes. Parents Day was approaching. Valia had already tried on her tutu. What could I do?

'Granny dear,' I whispered to my Granny, who was the Senior Teacher at the summer camp and would drop in to see me occasionally. 'Granny, ask Kira Ivanovna to have two herons in the swamp.' 'What herons? What swamp? What are you talking about?' Granny didn't understand. I explained, but she flatly refused to use family connections to get a Heron part for her granddaughter. However, two days later she came to see me with something fluffy in her hands. It was a tutu she had made for me in two nights. An array of pins sticking out of her mouth, she issued inarticulate commands, pinning and adjusting. I did everything as if in a dream, delirious with happiness. 'Okay, I'm sewing you up,' she pronounced, 'Hold your finger on your forehead, or I'll sew up your memory.'

On Parents Day benches lined a large lawn. Those who had no place to sit, settled down on the grass. My Mother came to see the show, bringing a bag of sweets. But I was completely in a daze. I waited to be called out. At last the accordion struck up and the Frogs started to jump. 'Herons!' the emcee announced. Valia and I advanced from opposite ends of the lawn. What a long lawn it was! I walked and walked with no end in sight. I flailed my arms and raised my knees high. My limbs refused to obey me. Still the lawn did not end... Finally, hurrah! I reached the edge. Mother grabbed me in her arms, kissed me all over, and popped a candy in my mouth. Later the photographer brought snap-shots of our concert: bears, rabbits, butterflies, our music teacher. And there were the herons. But... could that be me? Mouth half-open, stiff arms, shoulders pulled up to my very ears. And those legs with the toes pulled in! A pigeon-toed heron! I couldn't believe my eyes. I was sure I was a born ballerina. Why did Mother kiss me so much? That was my first great disappointment in life.

'Stop yelling, you're not the first and not the last to give birth,' the old nurse told me, a young woman in labour at the maternity hospital... Not the last — that's true. But why not the first? For each of us, it is the first time!

Each one of us is a great explorer, a pioneer, a discoverer of new lands and seas. So what if the sea I discovered already had a name, was teeming with bathers and plied by ships? It was mine... I discovered the sea in the first post-war summer in the resort town of Sochi, where Mother and I went to visit my uncle who was in hospital there. It was a warm summer evening. Mother, tanned, in loose black pants, with a magnolia in her hair. The local arboretum: palm trees, flowers, cypresses. Once, strolling through the arboretum, I heard the sounds of a foreign language, music, laughter. What was that? We followed the noise and came out into a lawn. Out in the open, an animated cartoon was being shown about a young deer just learning to walk. Its weak limbs kept sliding apart and he would fall all over himself. It must have been *Bamby*. The audience, seated on benches, consisted mostly of wounded men from the hospital, their friends and relations. White bandages, orange dots of cigarettes, and fire-flies gleamed in the dark. The air smelled of tobacco and magnolias, myriad of stars studded the southern sky, and somewhere close by, in the dark, I could hear the surf. My very first, inimitable South — a land which no longer exists anywhere on our planet.

Later, Granny took Mother's place. In the mornings, we would go to the beach. She got the idea she must teach me to swim. Once, as I was wading into the sea, unsuspecting trouble, she rushed in after me and, grabbing me across the midriff, dragged me into the deep. I started gulping water. I struggled desperately. 'You simpleton, you silly old fat-head!' I cried out, not knowing any other oaths except those I had read in Pushkin's fairytales. But my vigorous, still young Granny would not let go, and kept saying: 'Swim! I'm holding you. Swim!' The water kept getting in my mouth. I wriggled, trying to break free, and finally panicked, thinking that was the end: 'Brothers! Help, help!' And 'brothers' rushed to my aid. It was not so simple for them. They were mostly hospital patients basking in the sun. Responding to my plea, they hobbled on crutches to the water. My Granny, confused and embarrassed, released me and taking me by the hand waded toward the shore, followed by suspicious looks. I did not learn to swim that summer.

I discovered not only new lands and seas, but people's souls, even my own soul, with its secret nooks and dark crannies. Summer camp again. But now I was in my first year at school so I lived with Granny in the staff quarters rather than with the other children. I often went to the nursery group to help the staff put the children to bed. There I felt like Gulliver among the Lilliputians. Especially during 'dead hour' when the teacher went off somewhere and I was left in charge. 'Everybody shut your eyes!' I commanded in a steely voice. The children obeyed and lay motionless. Only their eyelids trembled a bit. One little Spanish girl, Carmen, kept looking at me with her wide-open black eyes. 'Carmen, close your eyes. I'll count to three,' I threatened. But her eyes wouldn't close. 'If you don't go to sleep, I'll make you stand at your bed!' Carmen kept gazing at me. I went up and lifted her light body out of the bed. The little girl's scalp was clean-shaven, mosquito-bitten and blotched with green antiseptic. She stood quietly. I put her back to bed and demanded: 'Shut your eyes.' Carmen stared at me. 'ALL RIGHT!' I blew up. 'Then I'll throw you over the fence!' I grabbed the wretched creature in my arms and carried her out of the room, passing between rows of petrified children. Dragging my victim up to the fence, behind which was a mound of black coal, I started swinging her, as if about to throw her over the fence. 'One...two...three...,' I counted. The girl was silent, only slightly pressing herself to me, watching me with her sad black eyes.

'What the hell are you doing?' I heard the teacher's alarmed voice behind me.

'She won't go to sleep,' I tried to explain, sheepishly. 'She refuses to obey. Won't shut her eyes.'

'As if we didn't have enough bosses around here! Your zeal will be the end of me,' the teacher exploded, snatching Carmen out of my arms.

I was never put in charge of the children again, but I often came to see Carmen. 'Hey, Carmen,' the children would call to her. 'She's come to get you again.' Carmen would come up to me and look into my eyes. I would hand her an apple or a candy, but she just stood there, motionless. I would press my present into her hand. I tried to talk to her, but, not knowing what to say, I kept asking her the same stupid question: 'What's your name?' 'Carmen,' she answered softly. 'Do you have a mother and father?' 'Yes,' she whispered. I had never seen Carmen laugh, cry, or get excited. She was an enigma. But so was I to myself. What on earth did I want from her? Why did I torment her? How many times I remembered with shame that far-off 'dead hour.' When we returned to Moscow in the fall, I went to the house for the Paris Commune factory workers, where several Spanish families also lived. They were refugees from the Spanish Civil War, of which there were many in Moscow at that time. Compared to other communal apartments, theirs seemed especially damp and squalid. But Carmen was nowhere to be found.

Only in childhood does life consist of self-contained moments which one lives through without any special purpose or perspective, just because they are there. In childhood, life is not a struggle, or an escape, or a chase, or a retreat, or a short-sighted rummaging in the cares of the moment. In one's childhood, every moment is a room which one explores in detail, lovingly. However brief, every moment has a middle, an outer edge, a dark nook, a cellar.

The refrain of my childhood was: 'Don't go outside the gate!' I was an obedient child and always — or almost always — listened to my mother and Granny. But even within our yard, the space was excessive. Even in my own stairwell, every floor was a new dimension. The ground floor was ours, lived-in and well-tread. Outside the door, to the right, was the red-haired tailless dog, Deska, who yammered every time somebody slammed the door. On the first floor the steps were much cleaner and the walls brighter. On the second floor I was seized by a sweet panic: foreign territory! The distance between steps seemed greater and it was harder to climb. I never dared enter the third floor — only peeked a couple of times. I never did go up there. Back I scampered, as fast as I could but treading softly, expecting at any moment a door to open and a cross voice to shout: 'What do you want here?'

When Mother first let me out of the yard, beyond the gate, I was at a loss where to go first: to the 'invalid' store for candy, or to the neighbouring yard where a house was being torn down, or to the kerosene shop. The delicious scent of kerosene! I could stand there for hours, inhaling that smell, watching the man in the huge yellow apron decant the precious liquid into customers' cans. The bubbling kerosene, the clanking lids, the clinking coins. That was my childhood, my native Polyanka Street.

My first school teacher was Lydia Sergeyevna. It seemed she always wore a blue silk dress with white polka dots. She sometimes came to our place to tell Mother about her love affairs. They would talk in whispers sitting with their feet up on the couch, but there would be an awkward silence whenever I happened to come in. Once, when Mother and I went to see her to the bus stop, she asked me to carry a stack of notebooks with our unchecked classroom work tied with a bright ribbon. I proudly carried the precious load, wishing I would meet some classmate, but alas I met nobody.

My first year at school... Fat, freckled Natasha Witensohn with her beautiful deep voice. She and I took part in a recitation contest. 'O Volga, my cradle!' Natasha recited with feeling. She was dressed in her school uniform: a white apron over a plain brown dress with starched white collar. From under her pleated skirt one could see her bare freckled legs with pink garters holding up stockings too short for her. Natasha won first prize and a book. I recited my favourite Krylov's fable, 'The Cuckoo and the Cock,' which earned me second prize and a postcard of a man with a scythe.

Quiet Natasha Vagurtova once took me home with her and confided in a whisper that last year her father had been arrested. As he was taken away, he told his wife: 'Lyuba, remember, I am innocent.' After that, her mother had been ill for a long time. Their room in the communal flat was confiscated and they were put in a curtained-off corner in a room which they had to share with another family branded 'enemy of the people'. The three of them: her mother, Natasha, and her elder sister lived there for a long time. When her mother returned from work, I was horrified to see her emaciated face and bulging eyes. 'Thyroid,' Natasha whispered to me as she caught my frightened glance.

I remember Galia Novikova, a mirthful girl I often went to visit in her tiny room in the old house nearby. She lived there with a lot of brothers and sisters. They all slept together on the floor and ate practically sitting on top of each other.

Galia shared a desk at school with the cranky Mila Sadovskaya. She often pilfered small objects from her classmates:

an eraser, blotting paper, a clean nib for a dip-pen. But when caught red-handed, she would get down on her knees and, theatrically pressing her hand to her bosom, would beg pardon, rattling off prepared lines.

In the fifth form we began to study the myths of Ancient Greece. The temples, battles, gods and heroes whose names I remembered with remarkable ease fascinated me. The only difficulty was the chronology. In Russian B.C. is indicated as 'before our era'. I would stare at the numbers, letters and dots unable to make any sense out of them. What did 'before our era' mean? I found it difficult enough to grasp what our era was. Imagination refused to be of any assistance. Why didn't they just write A VERY LONG TIME AGO? Surely that was enough? Yet even the dates did not succeed in dampening my enthusiasm for Greek myths. Particularly as they were taught by Anna Vasilievna. When she first made her stately entrance into our classroom, tall, imposing, her ash-grey hair drawn back into a bun, I thought she must have descended from Olympus. What Olympus was I already knew, first from Mother, then from Evgeny, who was Mother's husband for a while. Anna Vasilievna told us about gods and heroes slowly and calmly as befitted Olympus. As she moved silently up and down the rows in her long cherry dress and big white shawl all eyes were upon her. Cronos who swallowed his children, Zeus who overthrew Cronos, Hera, sister-consort of Zeus — she told us all about this in a way that left no doubt that she had been there. But who had she been in that unimaginable age before our era? Hera? Probably not. Hera was dreadfully vengeful and jealous. In the end I invented for her the role of a mysterious, nameless Olympian who stood above all the main gods and was indifferent to their games, passions and battles. The only thing not quite in keeping with her majestic image was the unexpectedly warm and welcoming smile which each of us longed to earn. All my time at home was spent on history, and in the lessons I was always putting up my hand (which you weren't supposed to do) or trying to catch her eye.

One day Anna Vasilievna did not come. They said she was ill and we had PT instead. Nor did she come for the next lesson or the one after that. Life became lacklustre. I found out where she lived and set off to visit her. How I had the nerve, I do not know. Clutching the scrap of paper with her address, I found the right street (fortunately not far away), went into the yard and, seeing a woman hanging up washing in the yard, showed her the address. She nodded briefly in the direction of a wooden building, but when I started up the steps, shouted 'downstairs'. Surely not in the basement? There was a smell of cats on the stairs and fried onion in the communal kitchen. 'Where is Anna Vasilievna?' I asked a shadow flitting along the dark corridor. 'This way, please,' the shadow replied in a young voice. We were soon in the dark, narrow room. On the bed lay a woman, her grey hair spread over the pillow. 'Who's that, Anya?' I heard Anna Vasilievna ask in a weak voice. I said my name. 'Oh, how nice, come over and sit down. Would you like an apple? Get an apple, Anya.' The girl flitted over to the sideboard. 'That's my daughter Anya. I've come down with pneumonia...' She used the Latin word. 'With what?' I asked, glad of the unknown word as a way of keeping up the conversation. 'With pneumonia, inflammation of the lungs.' 'When will you be back?' 'As soon as I can get up. You must go on reading. Would you like a book about the Trojan War?' 'No, thank you,' I said for some reason. 'We've got lots of books about the ancient world at home. Mother's husband is a philosopher. He knows everything.' 'Oh, well, that's great.' Anna Vasilievna looked at her daughter and smiled. Seeing how difficult it was for her to speak, I began to say goodbye. Anya put an apple in my hand and guided me along the corridor. 'Mother's eyes hurt, that's why we don't have the light on,' she said in parting.

Going up the same foul-smelling, rickety steps, I emerged into bright daylight. I walked home slowly, in a state of shock. What had surprised me so much? The slummy house? But we all lived in more or less similar conditions: in communal flats, amid soot and muck, rats and mice. But Anna Vasilievna, that proud and majestic Olympian, the supreme goddess. How could I ever have imagined her living in such a hole? How could I ever have imagined that this was where she came from each time to tell us about the feats of Hercules, Zeus, Hera and Hebe... 'You will say that fickle Hebe, / Feeding Zeus' eagle, / Did laughingly spill / The thunder-seething cup from heaven to earth,' she read in her deep, resonant voice. Unable to renounce the idea of Anna Vasilievna's Helenic origins, I decided to make her Persephone living in the underworld or at least Demeter who went down to visit her daughter in Tartarus. But no matter how hard I tried to adjust to this new version, it was no good. The dirty yard, damp basement, stinking corridor and dark room did not fit in with the noble-sounding Greek names.

At the end of term the door opened and in walked Anna

Vasilievna, serene and dignified, in the same dark cherry dress with a white shawl on her shoulders. She smiled her wonderful smile at us and said we were going to start a new theme. Then out streamed the magical names — Priam, Paris, Hecuba.

That was the class I loved, in which I spent six years and with which I had to part in 1952 when we moved. Our new home was in the same Zamoskvorechye district, but my previous life had ended. Another life began but I continued to live in my former life. Sometimes I'd wake up and did not understand where I was in relation to the door and window.

If anyone had said then: 'You must learn to adjust. This change is not the most terrible. There are worse times ahead,' I wouldn't have believed them. No one ever says such things, although that would have been the only consolation at the time.

Life cannot do without surgery. Every now and then it has to perform an amputation, taking away that which is habitual, dear, necessary. It leaves a gaping emptiness. It leaves pain, suffering, memory.

Childhood memories are capricious. The important, primary things are often forgotten. But small details, long past, can survive for decades. I remember waking up one morning to see something sky-blue in front of me. I reached out and felt it: silk. Blue silk hanging on the back of a chair. Little baskets with flowers against a blue background. A new dress. It was my birthday. I finally came to my senses, raised myself up on one elbow and saw the grinning face of a white-toothed black boy in a blue cap, made of wood. A weight was attached to his head, and the head rocked from left to right. He smiled at me for several years, rocking his head. Later something broke and the head stuck in one position. When we moved he wouldn't fit in any suitcase, so we had to decapitate him and pack the head separately from the body.

The meticulous memory of childhood. A memory for names. I remember the girl who slept next to me at summer camp outside Moscow — her name was Galia Sidorova. I was six. Every summer I went out of town with the kindergarten where my Granny held the strange job of Teachers' Advisor at that time. The kindergarten director was a loud-voiced, stocky woman from Siberia. Granny was responsible for educational work, because she alone had a college education at this kindergarten. Her obvious Jewishness and hot temper did much to complicate our lives — hers and mine. How many times I wished the earth would swallow me up when the director screamed at Granny who giggled nervously, crumpling the hem of her dress in her hand. The hem would climb higher and higher, until her pantaloons showed. Onlookers exchanged glances and snickered, while I sat red as a lobster, afraid to raise my eyes. I couldn't understand the reason for the hostility toward me and Granny, but I knew very well that if I did something wrong I would be punished more severely than the others. So, from the very first day at summer camp, I would shrink inside and wish that the summer was over. God, how I wished that everything would turn out alright somehow. I was always on my best behaviour. And yet...

Life was cruellest at night. For the night, a bucket was set out for us to use as a toilet. One bucket for both rooms. For some reason it always stood near the boys' room, and one of them would surely be on the alert. That bucket became the horror of my life. I would rather suffer until morning than use it. Once, having suffered for a while, I fell asleep. In my sleep I suddenly felt a great relief and warmth. When I woke up, I realised my sheets were wet. I broke out in a cold sweat. My brain started feverishly looking for a way out. Various absurd ideas came to mind. Noticing that my neighbour had woken up, I begged her: 'Galia, let's swap sheets when we make our beds. You know I'll get it in the neck because my sheets are wet, but nothing will happen to you.' Predictably, Galia refused. The old nurse called out to the teacher: 'Hey, look! Fruma's girl wet her bed. Fruma thinks she can teach everybody else but she has no time for her own grandchild.'

The teacher combed my hair, tied a big bow on my head and seated me in the middle of the veranda for all to see. On a clothes-line behind my back, my wet sheet was hung out to dry. I sat there with the pretty bow on my head until lunch time and everybody came to have a sneer.

In 1953, the year of the 'Jewish Doctors' Plot', there was a particularly severe outburst of anti-Semitism. I was about to enter the classroom; one of our girls (Zhuravleva, my memory prompts me immediately) stood in the doorway eyeing me with that same sneer. I went to my desk, feeling with every cell of my body that something was wrong. I didn't have a clue. I sat down at my desk, then noticed that my whole row was empty, I was completely alone while the other children all crowded into the other two rows. Zhuravleva questioned each as she came in the door. 'Are you with her,' she would query, pointing at me, 'or with us?' I was the only Jew in the class. I had no allies. Everybody was against me. They sat, pressed shoulder to shoulder, excited by their own unanimity and solidarity.

Lessons began. Yet not a single teacher asked what was going on. Everything proceeded as usual. Then our homeroom teacher launched into a tirade against the evil state of Israel, and then everybody turned around to stare me.

The days dragged on. Every day after class I expected to be beaten up. I knew the others were plotting something against me. When it happened, it came as a relief: at last! The girls formed a circle around me and started throwing me from one to another like a ball, giving me no chance to catch my breath. I didn't feel much pain or fear, only a numb resignation — and amazement that this was happening to me. At home I didn't say a word about it. I was afraid Mother would start walking me to school and back and the class would think I was a coward. When Stalin died the persecution stopped. One early morning we heard a wild knocking on the door, my stepfather went to open up, his eyes wide with fright. Our big, fat neighbour, half-dressed, burst in and embraced him. 'The doctors've been acquitted! Not guilty!' he repeated again and again, squeezing my stepfather. 'We're saved, my dear! Can you believe it!'

That day, our homeroom teacher did not come to class. She was so upset she developed German measles. Everybody took their usual seats and school life resumed its course.

Stalin was dead. Absent-mindedly, unhurriedly, I did my homework to the funeral music. Grandfather was bedridden after a heart attack. Mother and Granny spoon-fed him and helped him with the bedpan. When he heard of Stalin's death, he wrenched himself up and stood at attention, groaning as he held onto the back of a chair. No one dared argue with him. 'Why?' I asked myself. Why was Grandfather so shaken? A veteran member of the Bund (the Jewish Workers Union), he had been very critical of Stalin. He had even called him the source of all the Jews' sufferings. So why was Stalin's death such a misfortune? There he stood, slightly swaying, tears rolling down his cheeks.

Everyone behaved as though Doomsday had come, as if tomorrow the firmament itself would collapse. Complete eclipse. I was a bit ashamed of the excited curiosity I felt in those days of national mourning.

How I yearned for stability, to be able to trust those near me. I never knew what to expect from them. What frightening faces they might have and how cruel they might be towards each other. How often a trifle would set off a storm. There was my mother, her face contorted with rage, a kitchen knife in her hand, bearing down on Granny with terrible, senseless words.

'I'll kill you!' Mother shouted.

'Go ahead, kill me!' Granny shrieked hysterically. She would tear open her blouse, baring her scrawny neck.

I would crawl into a corner, biting my hands as I watched them. The world was collapsing. The previous life seemed to be over for good. The everyday scenes of the old life seemed like an unattainable happiness: drinking tea under the orange lamp-shade: Mother telling Granny about something, sitting cosily with one foot turned up in an armchair; Granny laughing her head off, like a girl, leaning over backwards, then doubling up and groaning: 'You don't say!' Her laughter would grow into a fit of coughing, and Mother would pause until she calmed down.

On Sunday, Grandfather's shaving ritual, which I watched from my bed. 'O the wonderful sea...' he would whistle as he sharpened his razor-blade on the belt tied to the handle of the wardrobe. Zzip-zzip-zzip: it was such a homey sound. Such an idyllic scene: Grandfather, in over-sleeves, his cheeks covered with soap, his neat movements, his little finger sticking out delicately, with blobs of stubble-grey soap-suds landing on the newspaper. Mother, lying next to me, reading aloud, mesmerizing me with the unexpected modulations of her voice and strange grimaces: now whispering, now shouting, eyebrows now knitted, now raised. I hardly listened to what she was reading, so fascinated was I by her manner. Everything she read seemed to bear a hidden, mystical meaning.

But now everything was falling to pieces. 'I'll kill you!' Mother shouted, her slender wrist twisted clumsily as she clenched the knife with her white fingers. How was I to know that she would never actually strike Granny and that those words were not meant to be taken literally, and that before me were two exhausted women who had survived four years of war? Days went by and life resumed its normal course, but I kept peering into their faces, asking myself: 'Did that all really happen? Do they remember?'

No matter how often those scenes took place, I couldn't get used to them. I craved stability, so that I could say about a person: 'He is incapable of a mean action. He will never do this. He will never say things like that.'

Now such a person is next to me. Every day with him is a gift. He has been with me for many years. It seems as though before I met him I had been standing on a slippery, mossy rock. Once, as a child, when we were spending the summer by the sea, I swam out on a huge black inner tube. It had sprung a leak and my only support was a slimy rock. I stood on tiptoes, my chin up high to keep the water out of my mouth. The moss kept shifting under my feet, it was alive. I felt as if I might lose my footing at any moment. The sun was blinding: I felt dizzy from the water shimmering around me. I felt that the slightest movement, even a sound, would make me lose my balance and I'd drown... Eventually I was rescued, but the feeling of standing on something precarious that might go under at any moment — that feeling remained until the day he appeared. He became my shore, my terra firma, my island of stability in this world.

He had been promised to me long ago, back in my early childhood. In the evacuation during the war I had a friend, a tow-headed boy of the same name. We were inseparable: we were bathed in the same tub, scrubbed with the same brush, lathered with the same bar of soap; we ate from the same slice of bread; we dressed in identical gray dresses with red trimming. When it turned out that he must leave for Siberia to join his father, we wept in each other's arms. We were dragged apart, with the dark bare table left between us. We were still in the same room, but apart, separated by something massive, oaken, insurmountable. It seemed to me then that the table was the cause of our separation.

We are probably born with the memory of joys, loves, losses, and partings of a previous life. We are born with this burden before we have accumulated our own. And every time our own new experience is, in effect, a recognition of that which subconsciously lived in us before our birth. Otherwise, how could I explain why, at the age of three, I was so deeply shaken by that parting? Why, in my childhood, I was so afraid for my family, especially Grandfather? Whenever we took a bus or train or tram, I always let him in ahead of me, fearing that he might not make it and the doors would shut on his foot. I never complained to him about the bullies in our yard, because I was afraid that he would stand up for me and get hurt. He was slight of build, moved lightly and always took up amazingly little space. To this day I can't understand where this self-educated Jew could have absorbed such grace and tact — a Jew reared in a poor family with many children, in which early on he became the only breadwinner. He spoke softly, but with a heavy Jewish accent, and his Jewishness was written all over his face so he always attracted attention.

I was especially afraid for him when Stalin launched the 'Doctors' Plot'. Once he was taking me to my music teacher. He was humming softly as we walked down the street. A man coming towards us knocked into him and hissed: 'You'll sing a different song soon enough, you dirty Kike!' I remember how terrified I was because, not having seen a single pogrom or even heard of one at my age, I clearly imagined the universal hatred of the people around us and their readiness to attack. What could it be but an innate memory of other horrors, as if I had lived another life before this one, or perhaps even several? Doesn't that explain why, when I hear someone sing an old Russian love song, I feel a sudden twinge of nostalgia for the life of the old nobility in all its details which, had I ever ventured to enumerate them, would seem like literature, but left unnamed are felt more keenly, as if they were your own past.

Isn't it for that same reason that when I hear the old names of Moscow streets — Prechistenka, Ostozhenka — my heart longs for the old Moscow, although its streets had been renamed by the time I was born. But come to think of it, had I lived in those old days I would probably have lived within the Jewish pale, and not in Moscow.

Somewhere on the border of my own and someone else's experience, I keep the memory (or is it only a memory?) of the evacuation from Moscow: the railroad station, the crowds and Father, in a shaggy jacket, holding me high up over his head so that Mother and Granny, whom he had lost in the crowd, would see me. I drift over people's heads, and suddenly Granny's piercing scream: 'Lara!' What happened next, I don't remember.

Memory is highly selective. A flash: I see the interior of a freight car, people bustling around a small stove; Granny peeling a baked potato, tossing it from hand to hand, blowing on it, salting it and handing it to me. I bite into it... The picture fades away, then continues, and I see myself running around in the streets of Kuibyshev during an air-raid, trying to catch the nervous spotlight in my hands. It keeps eluding me, so I pull off my mittens and try to catch it with my bare hands.

But how can I remember all that if I was only two years old? It seems that the border between one's own and another's experience is so shifting, so fluid, that you stop seeing the difference.

Perhaps for that reason I have always lived as though I had sustained losses in my previous life, and therefore I never took stability for granted but saw it as a great piece of luck and an indulgence. The older I got and the more roots I put down, the more vulnerable I became.

From my early childhood, life snubbed me, teaching me to be cautious. But how is it possible to learn to be mistrustful when only trust makes it possible to live in this world? Only trusting that the water will not flood us, the wind will not blow us off the face of the earth, and a neighbour won't stab us in the back — only then can we live, breathe freely, rear children, and sleep at night. In childhood, one trusts everyone, always ready to open one's heart.

How fortunate you are if you have a bosom friend living next door and you can see her whenever you feel like it. Once we sat in my room, munching honey-cakes. I was reading a funny verse I had just composed about our hateful teacher of needlework... I had written it the day before and was eager to share it with my friend.

> *The earth is rocked, the thunder roars:*
> *That's sure Paulina's on the loose.*
> *In her high-heeled shoes she stands*
> *With needlework clutched in her hands.*
> *She gives the lowest marks at school.*
> *She thinks any schoolgirl is a fool.*
> *But bottom marks are no big deal.*
> *We girls just laugh; our laughter's real.*

Natasha giggled: 'Make a copy for me. I'll read it to my

sister.' I copied it out while she stood behind me, chewing a honey-cake.

The next day we had a Young Pioneer assembly in class. I had joined the Young Pioneers only recently and was made a team leader. I was in seventh heaven and every now and then stroked the new stripe on my uniform sleeve. In the middle of the assembly, my friend Natasha, who was the class monitor, raised her hand, neatly planting her elbow on the desk.

'What is it, Natasha?' the homeroom teacher asked.

'Larissa Miller's written a verse about Miss Paulina. Let her read it out loud.'

'Read it,' the teacher said. I stared at Natasha, dumbstruck. Natasha looked straight ahead. Then rose, pulled a neatly folded sheet of paper out of her pocket — the one I had given her the day before, and declared: 'If she won't read it, I will.'

She read it, the girls giggled, and even the teacher could not suppress a smile. Natasha surveyed us calmly. 'I think it's quite clear,' she pronounced, 'that after this, Larissa Miller can hardly remain a team leader.'

The class fell silent. The teacher, confused, looked at me, then at Natasha, then at me again. Natasha sat down, rummaged in her briefcase, pulled out her pencil-box, got out a razor blade, and walked up to me.

'Stand up,' she commanded calmly. 'I'll remove the stripe.'

'Stop it, Natasha,' the teacher finally said. 'She'll do that herself, at home.' Natasha returned to her desk, put the razor blade back in the pencil-box, the pencil-box into the briefcase, the briefcase into her desk, put the desk-lid down, and leaned on it with her elbows. The meeting continued. My face was burning.

My mouth was dry. I couldn't understand what had happened, I couldn't find room for it, couldn't define it. The simple word 'traitor' came later.

'Everyone with a three for the term fetch your satchels and get in line,' said Lydia Sergeyevna. 'Now quick march after me to the cloakroom. You're going home. The others go quietly into the hall and take your places. You're going to watch a puppet show — *Ali Baba and the Forty Thieves*.'

We girls from 2-B with threes (there were no coeducational schools in those days) shuffled out behind our teacher, heads hung low. I tried not to look at the makeshift stage set up in the hall, but couldn't stop myself and through my tears I caught a glimpse of green spangled curtains and rows of benches where the girls with fours and fives were hopping up and down excitedly. My satchel felt like lead: inside was an end-of-term report with a three for maths. My only three for the term, and it had done me out of the puppet show, a happy homecoming and carefree winter holidays. There was just one week to go before the New Year, 1949.

I went outside and set off home without even saying goodbye to anyone. In our yard I met Mother who had left work early in honour of the school holidays. Seeing my woebegone expression, she began to interrogate me. I took out my report, showed her the three and told her everything. Next day Mother came home from work and put her bag down on the table. 'Guess what's in here,' she said. The bag was literally crammed with theatre and concert tickets, lots of them. The New Year celebrations were about to begin. Everyone got caught up in it:

Granny, Grandfather, Mother, even Mother's friends. I went to the operetta with Mother, to the opera with Grandfather, and to plays and the concerts with Granny.

'Happy New Year, dear country, glorious land of ours!' sang the golden letters on the ticket for a children's concert at the Young Pioneers Palace. The ticket showed 1949, the New Year, as a young man in a sheepskin jacket and fur cap with earflaps skiing towards Grandfather Frost who was carrying a sack out of which stuck Gaidar's book *Timur and his Team*. It was a splendid ticket indeed.

'First look at me / in the electric light, / Then turn it right off / And my tree will shine bright.' This little ditty was printed on the back of a ticket for the Columns Concert Hall. On the front was a rosy-cheeked, bright-eyed Young Pioneer in a white shirt and red tie holding a crimson star. The red of his banner, star and cheeks were fiery and festive. The holiday began in the morning. I went into the yard with my ticket to boast to the other children. They had brought theirs too and we argued about which was best.

One day I went out with my finest ticket of all, to a concert at the Central Club of Artists. It was a trick ticket. When you opened it, out popped a big bushy fir tree decorated with streamers, tiny animals and Grandfather Frost in a sledge with the Snow Maiden. Presiding over all this in the star-spangled heavens was Stalin's face. The ticket was passed from hand to hand. 'Let's have a look', said the boy next door, Yurka, who I'd had rather a soft spot for since he'd come back from the Suvorov military school for the holidays. I handed him the ticket not suspecting a trick.

The other boys crowded round him, inspecting it closely and whispering. 'Come here,' Yurka called, standing by our entrance to the stairway. 'Take a lick of that door handle.' 'Whatever for?' I said in surprise. 'You'll soon find out.' I hesitated. 'Take a lick,' Yurka wheedled. 'It's nice and sweet. Everyone else has had a go.' I was eager to do anything for him, so I licked the icy-cold metal door handle. In that severe frost my tongue stuck to the metal at once. Yurka and the boys ran off, laughing. I managed to pull my tongue away, leaving flecks of blood on the handle, then went home, forgetting all about the ticket and the concert. When evening came and Granny told me to hurry up, I realised that we weren't going anywhere. Yurka had gone off with the ticket. I told Granny I had lost it, then went to bed, pulled the blanket over my head and burst into tears. I cried for ages, wiping my tears on the sheet, until at last I fell asleep.

The next day there was another concert. And not just any old children's concert, but one at the Trade Union House. In those days grownups were allowed to accompany the children. It was so exciting to walk into the huge dark hall holding Granny's hand with music playing quietly and snowflakes drifting down. I took my seat and looked around. As if entranced by the magic snowstorm, the audience's chatter was hushed. Suddenly up went the lights and out boomed the master of ceremonies' voice — the show had begun.

My favourite number was the dance of the butterfly. A little ballerina dressed in something white and frilly fluttered onto the stage. She spun round in circles as she danced. One circle and her dress turned blue, another made it rainbow coloured, then chocolate brown, then yellow. The rays of the floodlight followed the little butterfly wherever she went, changing the colour of her wings. Each transformation was accompanied by appreciative 'oohs' and 'aahs'. Then the light went out and there she was again in her white costume.

There was one more number I always looked forward to: the two Nanais' wrestling match. Two tiny figures grappled with each other doing their darndest to pin the other fellow's shoulders on the ground. They rolled round the stage, falling down, bouncing up again, crouching in corners and whizzing over the floor. The audience roared: the children clapped like mad, jumping up and down and yelling advice. Suddenly one of the Nanais flew up into the air, felt boots and fur coat flashing past for the last time, and disappeared. There in place of the two stood a dishevelled, sweating young man, with two pairs of felt boots on his arms and legs. The audience was quiet for a moment, then burst into thunderous applause. No matter how often this number was shown, the effect was always the same: the roaring audience, the sudden hush, then the burst of applause.

After the concert everyone rushed over to the huge Christmas Tree to watch the lighting-up ceremony. 'One, two, three — light up, fir tree!' boomed Grandfather Frost, with a blow of his staff, and the tree lit up. This was greeted by the usual chorus of 'hoorays' and then at last Grandfather Frost asked: 'Who's going to recite us a poem?' Me, of course. I knew so many poems I could go on reciting till the cows came home. So out I went and began: 'Little Moscow girls have two pigtails, little Uzbek girls have twenty-two...' or 'We children live in a happy land and a happier land there cannot be...' or 'At this late hour Stalin is thinking of us all...' Then Grandfather Frost took me by the hand and gave me a present from the tree. After that there was dancing. I was always a little snowflake in a white skirt and white crown.

At one such party a prince in tights and a golden jacket came up and asked me to dance. He had a shining crown on his head and stayed with me all evening. We went to get presents together, and when my paper packet burst and the sweets and gingerbread fell out and the tangerines went rolling all over the floor, my prince rushed to pick them up. I felt like Cinderella at the ball and was in such a hurry that I couldn't get my arm into the sleeve of my coat. Quick, quick. He's waiting. Now I'm ready. But where was he? Looking round, I saw a tall thin girl standing next to me. Her face seemed familiar. 'I'm Tanya,' she said. 'That's your prince,' laughed a tall young woman, very like Tanya, Tanya's mother. We walked towards the exit. Granny chatted to Tanya's mother, and Tanya tried to talk to me, but I hardly heard what she was saying and made some vague replies. We parted company at the bus stop.

Very often the winter holidays dragged on due to illness. At the end of the holidays I usually got a sore throat or earache, or swollen glands and a high temperature, and gladly let myself be tucked up in bed. One day I found myself standing on the table, pointing at the wall and whispering: 'A red ribbon, there's a red ribbon on the wall'. Mother and Granny exchanged horrified glances. 'Agree with her,' Granny whispered. 'When a child is delirious, you must agree with it.' What happened after that, I don't remember. Later I learnt that I had scarlet fever.

Being ill as a child was sheer bliss. It meant fever and feeling a bit dizzy. An anxious and caring mother who didn't go to work and made you jelly and put mustard poultices on your back. Being ill meant that they read to you and when your temperature went down they'd let you have books, pencils and drawing paper in bed. Being ill meant drinking a nice sweet cough mixture prescribed by the excellent district doctor Bukharin, the excellent children's doctor, a kindly and perpetually tired elderly woman, who disappeared suddenly and completely in the early fifties. I later learned that she had been arrested because of her unfortunate surname, although she had nothing whatever to do with that 'enemy of the people', the ex-leader Nikolai Bukharin.

Trying to recall all the holiday entertainment made my head woozy. My favourite plays were *The Twelve Months* and *The Blue Bird*. I had seen them a hundred times and would gladly go again. What I liked best in *The Blue Bird* was the Other Kingdom and Running Nose played by a young woman with a big red nose who ran round the stage sneezing all the time. And in *The Twelve Months* I liked the storyteller in striped trousers. He came out before each act and jigged up and down in a funny way, chanting something like 'bim-bam-boogy, boogy-baziloogy'. I also remember a play called *Snowflake* that I saw with Granny at the Children's Theatre. Snowflake was a poor little black boy, oppressed and downtrodden. He was tormented and persecuted by the white Yankees in hateful America. How I wished I could save that little boy, spirit him away to Moscow, give him a nice warm home and comfort him!

What else did I see? I tried to reconstruct everything right from the beginning and suddenly saw clearly the school hall, the green spangled curtains and the large notice in flowery handwriting: *Ali Baba and the Forty Thieves*, the most interesting, desirable and inaccessible show of all, the forbidden fruit of my childhood.

But life went on: home, vacation, school again. I see myself bursting out of school, out of the dark stuffiness into the airy March daylight. My head is hot. I remove my fur cap and carry it in my hand. All the roofs are dripping. I put my head under the falling drops, then my hand, my collar, my cap. The fur on the cap sticks together, and I press them down in one direction, then in another. I wash my galoshes and briefcase under the slender stream. My wet briefcase glitters in the sun, as drops of water fly into my face. The pencil-thin stream crashes down on my hand, on the asphalt, on the fur of my cap, now ringing loudly, now muffled... When I get home, I discover that all my schoolbooks are drenched, and the ink in my notebooks has run. I arrange the books on the radiator, and start a new notebook. Brand-new, dazzling white, it is impressive. I remove a piece of clean blotting-paper and put it under my left elbow. I touch the nib of the dip-pen to see if it is clean. I dip it into the ink and carefully write the first words on the clean page: 'March 20th.' I solemnly vow to write without a single mistake or blot, and my hand trembles with excitement.

What a bright day it is outside! Every little spot on the windowpane stands out. The layer of dust is clearly visible on the marble inkstand, in the centre of which stands a white owl with green eyes — a night-light. Actually, its eyes are now dull from dust. I rub the dust off with my finger. My finger is grey. I rub all the dust off the owl and the marble inkstand. I run my finger down the oilcloth on the table, then go up to the piano.

What unlimited scope! I run my finger down the dusty candlestick, then write all over the piano lid in a sprawling script: 'The Twentieth of March.' I raise the lid and write the date inside. The dust particles dance in a shaft of light. I put the piano-score of *Evgeny Onegin* — a fat brown volume — on the stool, sit on it, and start practising. I run through the etude several times, then separately with my right hand and my left hand, then run over the keys at random. Then I pull the score from under myself, open it, play the first bars, leaf through the pages, start in the middle, singing to the tune.

I enjoy leafing through piano scores. I place in front of me some pages that are falling apart. They cannot stand up, and slump into my hands. I hold them up with my left hand, groping around the keys with my right. Someone has marked the fingers between the lines, drawn a legato in pencil, crossed something out. Someone has obviously struggled with this piece before me, confusing fingers, breaking up the legato. The yellow pages are crumbling, but the music has survived. It's so wonderful to find the keys you need, strike them and discover how the sounds, hinging onto each other, give birth to something that takes your breath away. The secret meaning of these harmonies is still hidden to me, but they move me, make my heart yearn. A mystery. I am on the threshold, as though peering into someone's window, while someone inside waves to me, smiling, calling. I go in — and find myself on the outside again, again rows of windows, and again I peer into them. Again someone waves and calls to me from inside. I enter — and find myself on the outside again.

I keep circling, trying to get inside. Impossible. I strike the keys, they respond, but the answer is evasive.

I violate the purity of a new page, but my efforts boil down to a spelling exercise.

I walk through a spring day, a ringing, babbling day. The day is chattery and yet it does not blurt out its innermost secrets.

The houses too keep their secrets. Here's the old one-story building where my music teacher lives. A window is open letting out laboured music, or rather a slow, uphill labour, riddled with mistakes. I go up to the window and peer into the room. I hear my teacher's voice: 'One-and-two-and...' I can see the black piano. I tap on the pane, as agreed. She doesn't hear me. I tap louder. She calls out to someone and I see a small figure run out of the room to open the front door. I hurry into the courtyard where the front door is. The marquee is held up by an ornate lattice of wrought iron. Bare ivy vines cling to the iron lattice. The thick trunks of ancient trees block the view from the windows, as though in collusion with the house.

But even inside a strange house, I fail to penetrate the mysteries of its life. Here we are in the home of an old, decrepit lady musician. Our music teacher has brought us here for an audition. The crowded corridor is dominated by a tall, clouded mirror in a carved frame. We leave our hats and mittens on the mirror table and enter the dimly lit room, half of which is occupied by a grand piano. The room smells of musty old books and medicines. An old woman sits in an armchair in a long skirt and felt-boots. Her legs are paralysed. To her left is a round table with medicines, books, and a tin of lolly-pops. We play the piano while she listens intently. Then suddenly her sonorous voice breaks in. She makes a few remarks, asks us to repeat the same piece, and beats the time with her gaunt, freckled hand.

While others play, I look at the paintings on the walls and try to guess what people and places are shown there. There's a portrait of a young beauty. Could it be this same old woman? And what are those cliffs and sea in the picture in the corner?

It's all so mysterious: the steps at the entrance door, the half-dark room, the wrought-iron lattice with the ivy, the old woman with her stentorian voice, the spring thaw, the blinding sun, the dancing dust particles in the shaft of sunlight — what am I to do with all this?

I can touch everything, but cannot penetrate it, cannot reach its inner meaning, its core, cannot solve its riddle.

The old bookcase of my childhood. A multitude of books. Some are without covers. I leaf through them, sniff them, study the pencil marks in the margins, start reading — and plunge into another world. I am carried away by strange passions and lives. I read until my eyes ache. Then shake myself free of another's life with difficulty. Two shelves are devoted to pocket-sized volumes of poetry. I pick one out at random, choose one of the shorter pieces and read: 'I've lost all to a vengeful God...' Lost. Vengeful. The words are cryptic. They mesmerise rather than frighten me.

I open a thick notebook, take a pencil, pick the eraser with the sharp pencil, — undefinable, mysterious feelings fill my heart. Finally, I put down the first few words: 'There was a house-warming party next-door...' I write on and on, excitedly, reluctant to stop writing, speeding towards the end. It's a simple, short story about a certain family, their quarrels, reconciliations, birthdays, bad school marks, and a happy ending. When I finish, I give a sigh of relief. My eyes scan the lines. Is that what I intended to write? I don't know. Remarkable how clean it turned out to be. Not a single crossed-out word. I could erase anything I didn't like. It's thrilling to hold in your hands the whole thickness of the written pages: look how much I've created!

But the greatest pleasure is still ahead: I will take this story to the most cherished house of my childhood. That's where my father's friends live. Mother and I inherited them from my father.

I always remember that house in winter: the lane blocked with snowdrifts, the small wooden houses snowed under. The long wooden staircase, with a brush standing at the foot of it. Mother and I brush the snow off our boots and go upstairs. We push one of the doors open and find ourselves in a tiny anteroom where an omelette with slices of black bread is being cooked on a tiny electric stove. The anteroom is separated from the rest of the room by long drapes. We pull the drapes apart and enter the room. In the middle stands a wooden pillar extending from the floor to the ceiling. It seems as though this pillar had managed to lift the roof high enough to make room for the two old people. And they are so glad to have this space that they lavish all their love on it: hanging bookshelves and pictures on the walls, even bringing in a piano. The top of the pillar is intricately ornamented, while lower down it supports more bookshelves.

People work in this room, writing books about authors and musicians. I like the inhabitants of this room. I like to read my own stories to them. Aunt Liza sheds a few tears as I begin reading and Uncle Alyosha softly taps the table with his fingers. 'Well,' he says when I finish, 'good for you, my dear girl. Keep it up, Lara!'

Aunt Liza embraces my head and presses it to her bosom. Uncle Alyosha and I curl up in a corner of the couch. I settle down in his lap and we invent plots. He begins, then I continue, or the other way round. He thinks up something incredible, then breaks off at the most interesting point: 'Okay, you go on from here,' he says.

Then Aunt Liza places a small table by the couch, and we drink tea.

When I am ready to leave, I hug Uncle Alyosha and whisper: 'I love you both, I do.'

That home is no longer there. Neither are its inhabitants. Not that they died. It all ended much earlier: when they had their works published and moved to a fine apartment, they became self-important and house-proud.

But the cherished little house is still alive in my memories. I mount the nonexistent steps of the long-ago demolished house and ask Aunt Liza: 'Could you play the Griboyedov waltz for me?' Uncle Alyosha takes the ancient score off the music stand and inscribes it, imitating Griboyedov's hand: 'To my darling Lara.'

...It's March again. The birds are chirping and my eyes are smarting from the dazzling light. I'm walking with my little son along the streets of my childhood. Here is the little lane where I used to go for my music lessons. Which is the window I used to knock at? This one? No, I think it's that one. You can't tell now. The windows are boarded up, and so are the doors. The house is ready for demolition. The boarded-up windows are a silent rebuke. I never did solve their mystery. But I remember the breath and smell of this house, I remember how the keys of my teacher's grand piano would sometimes get stuck, and how she would seize my wrist and shake it, demanding: 'Loosen up!'

'Loosen up,' the young music teacher tells my son who is trying hard to scale the same piano scores I once did. He tumbles down, then presses on.

Spring is a strange season. There is increasingly more sky and sunlight, making more glaring the imperfections of the world as well as our own inadequacies. Spring casts light on everything, catching us unawares, and not in our best guise. Look at this world — aggressive, loud, all littered and sick. Look at them, I mean ourselves, who made it that way and then demanded an answer from the Almighty for all the misfortunes. But the Almighty is 'duty-bound' insofar as he created us, while we, having fancied ourselves to be his co-authors, keep creating only all sorts of messes.

It's warm outside, fluffy clouds float lazily over concrete apartment blocks, while around them, from under melting snow protrude all manner of leavings from daily life, lavishly lit up by the sun — empty milk cartons, jars, cans, fish tails, chicken bones, dirty bandages.

Come on, sun, splash brighter,
Bake us all with your golden beams!
Hey, comrade, ripen up more life,
Don't hold back, step to it!

They used to sing this song a few decades ago when we all believed that man was born for happiness, 'like a bird for flight'. Who wouldn't wish to stand guard at night in the magic garden to track down the Firebird that comes for golden apples every

night, and catch it by the wing? If gardens have become scarce,
Firebirds still come down to earth from time to time. Everybody
knows that, especially in childhood. To this day I keep a little
book, written and drawn especially for me by my best friends
Uncle Alyosha and Aunt Liza, which they gave me in the spring
of 1947 for my seventh birthday.

> The Firebird now tells the tale,
> Listen, lovely maiden fair,
> Listen to my little song,
> Just like me, you'll sing along!
> Here's a feath'ry gift for your good name,
> It's not just a feather, it's fire, flame!

To the left of the verses the Firebird flaunted its beauty,
with a crown on its head and a long multi-coloured tail; to the
right, a burning feather, spitting sparks. The Firebird promised
to me in my childhood would indeed come, bringing wonderful
presents. Once it appeared in winter and, lighting up everything
around, gave HIM to me. It seemed heaven had descended to
earth. It seemed... well, there was much I imagined at the time.
But Spring came, his inimitable velvety voice suddenly shrivelled
and started to sound wheezy and disaffected. 't's nothing,' I
consoled myself. 'Spring is a hard time for asthmatics. Look how
many irritants there are: down, pollen, sunlight.' But the exacting,
merciless sunbeam dispelled my delusion, leaving me no hope.
'Look,' it demanded, 'don't turn away.'

I looked and saw... my best friend's cosy kitchen. At the
table, HE, she and I. I had shown up without phoning first,

surprising them both. I had been worried after a telephone conversation the night before, a conversation consisting mostly of pauses and his strained coughing. 'He's sick,' I had said to myself over and over again. 'An attack of asthma.' And that day, listening to HIS voice rich in velvety modulations, and seeing his happy smile, I was convinced that he really was sick, 'wondrously sick,' but — not over me. For me it was all over. That kitchen drowning in sunlight, decorated with a pretty lampshade and a funny picture on the wall, became the site of my execution, which was carried out by my best friend with the help of her black, green-eyed cat called Mao. Having strolled around the kitchen and rubbed against our legs, Mao jumped up onto HIS knees. Wary of undesired consequences (the fluffy cat could provoke the asthma), my friend leaned over and with a careful, solicitous, intimate movement took the cat off HIS knees. This gesture proved fatal for me: my head rolled off its shoulders. There still played the likeness of a smile on my face; the lips twitched, pronouncing some words or other, but the sentence had been carried out.

Spring is the time of catastrophes. It was in spring that I first witnessed the agony of death. Granny was dying. She cried out horribly and fell on her back, twitching and bending as if a current was running through her, then abruptly she stretched out and quieted down. I held her still-warm hand, familiar down to the last tiny cuticles on the fingers, and caught her breathing, dying away. On the night table lay a little red pin cushion, a spool of thread and my jacket, she was going to tighten the buttons on it. I took the shocked children out for a walk and vacantly followed after them along a golden field of dandelions, along the slope of a ravine, multicoloured with lungwort, across a rickety little bridge over a brook. The nightingales were singing, the cuckoo cried; everything that is supposed to be happening in Spring was happening. When we came home, the bed was empty — so as not to distress the children, they had taken Granny away to the morgue. She died in May, the same month in which sixty-five years before, she had given birth to my mother. Three years after Granny's death, my mother died. That also happened in Spring, in March — the same month in which she had brought me into the world. For my birthday I would get mimosa, and mother would get lilacs.

> Lilacs, birthday, celebration, phone calls,
> Diseases, exhaustion, partings, wreaths...
> Bouquets at the beginning, bouquets at the end...
> We live, our faces gradually changing,
> Changing almost beyond recognition...
> Oh, eternal saying: 'Don't waste time,'
> That very time, that doesn't exist -
> That weightless time of lost years.

Mother's last day was not sunny, but light streamed from everywhere — from leftover snow, puddles, rivulets, trees. The light was greedily snatched up by the windows in buildings. One of these windows in a hospital was to be her last. Through it she saw a large old tree and birds flying by. She loved to look at them while there was still hope. But on that day her ashen face expressed nothing besides exhaustion and deathly torment.

Spring is where beginnings and endings meet, the time of

their fraternisation. My younger son, marked with an abundance of golden freckles, was born in early Spring. And four days before his appearance on earth, Grandfather died in his ninety-second year. In springtime something happens to the thread of life. It becomes almost visible in the spring light, gets tangled, quivers, stretches tight, grows thin, and breaks. But then another thread — also fragile, but flexible and hardy — appears to replace it.

In Spring stereotypes break and people get out of ruts. Even if it does not happen in springtime, but later, Spring conceives such changes. I remember how in childhood I would feel butterflies in my stomach in anticipation of a change in fortune: the end of the school year, the last homework test, the inevitable exams, promising triumph or defeat.

In Spring suitcases with the label 'summer' would be produced from the attic, and an inventory of my summer things made. Watching Granny thread a small needle, make a little knot, sew labels on my pants and T-shirts, I fell into anguish and shed 'tears unknown and unseen'. Because all this heralded my departure for summer camp and life in a' healthy collective': reveille, retreat, the hated 'dead hour' in broad daylight, when you close your eyes and pretend to be asleep listening to the voices that carry from freedom, and you dream of growing up and living to that time, when... further on your thoughts get mixed up and sleep comes.

Spring is a time of secret ambitions, of dizzying and hazy schemes. Your former life begins to get on your nerves, like a tiresome chore, urging you to kick, tear yourself away, fly off to the pampas, or at least a pond outside Moscow to watch a frog wedding. Spring provokes vacillations and outbursts, playing a

game with you like the one in Chekhov's The Little Joke: *'This
way, this way!' you hear above your ear, and you turn — no one
there. It was just a branch that snapped, ice that cracked, a
sunbeam sliding along your cheek. A flimflam. It's time you got
used to it and didn't swallow the bait. But if you didn't swallow
it, would life be worth living?*

*In early Spring your life heels over, gets dislodged, its rhythm
breaks, and you feel compelled to review the very foundations of
existence.*

> *Everything will shift a little more -*
> *A sunbeam more to the right, a bird farther south,*
> *And the listing will grow more distinct,*
> *And the book will slide off my knees.*
> *My gaze will shift, the lines change position,*
> *Everything will move from its habitual spot,*
> *And I find myself at an angle*
> *To that which is my path and home...*

*Paradoxically, it is precisely in times of high water that you
find yourself aground, on starvation rations, that you come to
nought, your reserves of vitality growing scarce and vitamin
deficiency sets in, the deficiency of that matter upon which
depends the next move, the round circuit in the spiral of your
life. And no help is forthcoming from any quarter. Seek the
missing elements yourself, like a dog seeks out a healing herb.
But even to start looking you need energy, and where will it
come from in your state of vitamin deficiency? Problems,
problems — in fact there's only one problem, really. Its name is*

'I'. That same 'I' that compels the artist to sign his canvas, and a poet to sign a sheet of paper with his verse, as if calling out: 'Here I am, Lord, all of me, like an open palm. I have no secrets from You and no strength to create anonymously, like the medieval masters. It may be arrogance on my part, or else the need for Your judgement, for Your defence, is too overpowering.'

'I' is a strange creature, endlessly demanding something for itself and endlessly striving for freedom from itself, to lighten its soul, to speak out, cast off part of its burden, be left free and easy, grow transparent, like a spring day through which clouds swim and birds fly. The world is needlessly weighted down with wars, epidemics, natural disasters, even without them life is an ordeal, and any human being, if only his or her soul isn't asleep, is a point of pain and a centre of tension: insult stings, pity torments, conscience tears to pieces, passion burns, tenderness chokes. From birth each of us is sentenced to death, and each of us is fated to spend his or her life tangled in the myriad of multicoloured drapes with which the Lord has concealed from us THAT WHICH HAS NO NAME. In Spring the drapes, the MAYA, become almost translucent, but only a celestial ultramarine shines through. And nothing else. Save me, MAYA. Support me the way the salt water in the Dead Sea buoys one and all. Let me get across this crisis zone without sinking.

Spring is the time of passions consummated through the final expiration and subsequent resurrection. It gives us a chance to glimpse the Promised Land from which we are banned. This is for the better, for if we settle there it will disappear. Any settled life takes away freedom. As soon as you stop, petty worries latch on like mosquitoes at a camp site. You cannot reach your *destination, you can only keep going. Fanning yourself with a small green branch, like the one that once, long ago, stood on my desk in a glass jar. It was Spring. A Rachmaninoff piano concerto played on the radio. The windows were wide open. There was one day left until final exams. I looked in the book at a larynx in cross-section, a hard and soft palate and other relevant organs, but phonetics lived its own life, and I my own. Mine was filled with Spring smells and daydreams, Rachmaninoff exuberances and peals, and poplar down floating in through the window.*

Papa Misha

When I was four, I liked to play with an old photograph of myself, age one, sitting in Father's arms. I liked to crumple the photo, then smooth it out and draw all over it with colour pencils. Mother and Granny would rescue the victimised photo, but I would find and torment it again.

'Your father went to the front as a volunteer,' I was told. 'He had poor eyesight. He was killed when he stepped on a land mine... Papa Misha loved you very much,' Granny would often repeat. 'He held you carefully like a crystal vase. He had long musical fingers.'

When I grew older I was sorry I had drawn all over the picture in which Papa Misha is holding me with his 'long musical fingers'. I studied his hands on that photo for so long that it seemed as if the fingers were slightly trembling. I pored over his face, closely cropped hair, glasses, his smile, and myself in overalls with tiny buttons, the vase, the mirror, the rug — the whole faraway background of my pre-war childhood, in which Papa held me like a crystal vase.

What else do we have left from that life? Here is a snapshot of Mother and Father on the shore of the Black See. That was before me. Mother has on a broad-brimmed straw hat and a striped bathing suit. She has a deep tan. Father is thin and bespectacled. They lay on the sand at the water's edge, laughing, splashed by the coming waves.

Here is a small photo from his 1934 identification card for the *Tagil Workers* daily. Another shows him in army uniform. He is sitting on a chair; Mother is standing beside him, they are smiling at each other.

I was told very little about Father at home. I only knew that he loved poetry, that he was shy, tall and thin, and that he wore glasses I tried to pull off his nose whenever he took me in his arms. He wouldn't let me and I'd scream with vexation.

How strange it was to read my own name in his letters from the front: 'We will defeat the Nazis, and I'll return to my dearest Lara.'

At one time I had the feeling that Father was alive, and I searched the faces in the crowd, trying to find him. It's strange how I came to miss him. Almost none of the girls in class had fathers. My family was actually larger than many others, besides Mother, I had Granny and Grandfather. There were also Father's sisters and a brother, but we did not see them very often. And yet, I was waiting for him to come back, I searched for him everywhere, I composed stories about him. I missed him most acutely when quarrels broke out in the family, and also when Mother was dismissed from the *Red Army Men* newspaper, when she and I roamed the streets, reading 'Help Wanted' notices, and when I was harassed by the other children in the yard.

I liked to go and visit Father's home in the Arbat where his relatives lived after the war, in the long building with a round tower. Even today I show this house where none of my relatives live any more, to my children: 'Look, there's Papa Misha's house.'

I never dreamed about my father as a child. The first time was when I was in my early thirties. There were many things I wanted to tell him, but my lips wouldn't oblige because we had very little time: he was wounded in the temple. There was a trickle of blood coming out of his wound. Someone was trying to stop the blood, but it kept coming. It was a mortal wound. He was pale but overjoyed to see me. He held my hand and kept asking me something in a feeble voice. I wanted to answer — but suddenly woke up. That was terrible: My father had disappeared — my father for whom I'd waited for so many years, found at last, and lost again. I never did manage to tell him anything.

That dream haunted me for a long time.

Thirty-six years after his death, I happened to meet Nahum Melman who was with my father at the front and who spoke to him the day before he died. He told me something about him that I did not know. He told me he had first met him in Kuibyshev, during the war.

Father desperately wanted to go to the front, but they wouldn't let him because of his poor eyesight. Finally, he found a way of circumventing the medical commission by joining an army newspaper. There he was an assistant to the managing editor and spent much time at the printing house. He was wildly overworked. Whenever he had a free moment, he would hum something quietly or recite poetry. He knew an awful lot of poems by heart and could recite them for hours. 'He lived on poetry and music. Or rather, in poetry and music. It seemed that music and poetry had been written for him alone,' Melman told me.

He also loved Mother to distraction. That love cost him his life. Once, when he learnt that a car would be going from the frontline to Moscow, he and his friend Anatoly Mednikov decided to make the trip to see their families. Business trips to Moscow were usual for editorial staff. Their absence could have passed unnoticed, because a bomb had hit the printing house and the paper's issue had been suspended. My father, as a hopelessly civilian man, could see nothing wrong in his reckless action. In Moscow, he spent some time looking for Mother. As a journalist working on the *Red Army Men* magazine at the time she was often sent on assignments.

He spent three or four days in Moscow. From there, he sent a radiant letter to Yadrin, where his sisters and parents lived at the time: 'My dearest ones! A miracle has happened! I'm writing to you from Moscow! And guess who is sitting next to me! Bela!!!' I read this letter only recently. It was given to me by my father's sister shortly before her death. He had been close to her. Mother, however, had rather strained relations with her in-laws. So I did not see them very often.

Thus Papa Misha began to return to me. He returned through his friends' stories: fellow-students at the Literature

Institute, colleagues at *Literaturnaya Gazeta*, and at the army newspaper at the front.

Melman told me: 'On my birthday Misha gave me a book of poems by Pasternak in a blue dust jacket. I did not want to take it because it was the only book he had with him at the front. "Take it," he insisted, "I remember the whole book by heart, but you don't." '

Many years later, I began trying to trace his movements. I spoke to those who knew him back in the war days. I spoke to Mednikov, the man with whom he lived through the most terrible period of his life. With great pain, he recalled the events of 1942.

Their unauthorised trip to Moscow was reported to the Political Commissar.

He had the two court-martialled. Stalin had recently issued a decree on strengthening discipline in the army. Father and Mednikov were sentenced to death. 'The court session was held in a large peasant house,' Melman recalled. 'I saw Misha from the back. His head was shaven. He was in his great coat but without his belt and half-belt. The half-belt had been cut off, the belt taken away. So were his glasses. I remember his last words. He said he only wanted to be able to look honestly into his daughter's eyes.'

After the court-martial, the two convicted men were taken to a cabin, which served as a jail, and later to the Kaluga Central Prison. There they spent 90 days in the death cell. The cell was on the second floor. It was packed with assorted convicts. Every night someone would be taken away for execution accompanied by hysterical outbursts from the doomed and those who were left.

The others looked upon Father and Mednikov as oddballs
— they spent their time teaching each other. Father would give
lectures on literature, music and cinema, while Mednikov taught
him mathematics and other sciences. The two even celebrated
his birthday, and father gave him half of his daily ration of grain
soaked in water, the only food they were given.

Three months later, the convicted men were called down
to the first floor. They did not know what awaited them. As
soon as the sentence was passed, an appeal was sent to President
Mikhail Kalinin, but his decision was not known.

In order to avoid hysterical scenes in the communal cell,
they started taking the condemned men first to the preparatory
cell on the first floor. The convicts knew of course where the
other cell was. So did my father and his friend. Their walk down
seemed interminable.

More than forty years later, Mednikov was telling me in a
trembling voice about those endless minutes: the corridor, the
stairs, another corridor. The fateful door was coming closer and
closer. Would they be pushed behind that door, or would they
go past? They were led past the door. Their appeal had been
won, the death sentence commuted to ten years in prison camp,
including service in a penal battalion at the front.

The two friends were sent to a camp outside Yoshkar-Ola
(near the Volga), and from there to the front. They were taken
in a freight train through Moscow. The train stood in Moscow
for several hours, and miraculously Papa saw Mother again. That
was last time they saw each other. I don't know if he told her
what he had gone through. There is no one I can ask. In a letter
to his parents and sisters, he said he had not written all those

months because he had been wounded and laid up in a hospital. But the letters he sent Mother have not survived.

Mednikov told me he behaved courageously. Only in the camp, when he had nothing to eat, he had begun to get nervous that he wouldn't be sent to the front. But he was sent there eventually, and even miraculously met Melman again.

Part of the summer, the whole autumn up till the end of November, the two convicted men spent writing the history of the 326th division. The Commissar liked them and ignored the fact that they'd been convicted. By November, the history had been completed, the Commissar was called to Moscow, while my father and Mednikov were sent to a reserve company.

Father was killed in the very first battle. This happened on 26 November 1942. He was 28.

Now I understand why so little was said about Father at home, and why even his war-time friends were not mentioned. My relatives were afraid I might learn something not meant for my ears. They were afraid for my sake, for the sake of my future.

Throughout my childhood, I only heard: 'Papa Misha went to the front as a volunteer and was killed by a land mine.' As long as I remember myself, I remember these words. Many times in my childhood I imagined a huge snow-covered field and Papa Misha, alone, almost blind, in his glasses, making his way over that field. Then suddenly an explosion. What happened next I could not imagine, so at that point my fantasy would break off, and I'd start all over again: the white field and my father's solitary figure slowly walking towards his death...

Finally I had my father's last letter in my hands, his letter from death row addressed to his front-line friends:

My dear friends,

The time for parting is not far away. Perhaps it will happen when I least expect it. So, while there is still time, I want to tell you all.

Everything that has happened is dreadful, I don't know whether I'll be able to bear it all, I'm afraid I may not. All too often thoughts of my little daughter, my wife, my mother, rush thundering into my mind. What a terrible misfortune has befallen them. Their father, husband, son — a deserter, a criminal! How can I prove it's not true? What can I do? They'll send me to a forward position and I will die ignominiously, never having expiated my crime with my blood. What hero I am! They'll put me in prison, a death sentence in itself! I so much wanted to work with you in whatever capacity. They will not entrust any work to me now, you can be sure. In short, it's the end, the totally absurd, unexpected end. That's how things are, my dear friends.

However long I have left to live, perhaps very little, I will always think of you, brothers. You're the only people who understand, who believe, that I'm not a deserter or adventurer. I'm the wretched victim of that ill-fated confusion. I'll always remember your sympathy and concern for me in these difficult days, I'll remember all the good times we had together over the last two months.

Do explain to those who remember me that I am no criminal, that everything was a terrible mistake on my part. If there is an address of any kind for me give it to anyone who wants to write to me. Letters will be the only joy in my life. Explain to everyone that I fell victim to my love of Moscow, a love we all share. It never occurred to me that, precisely in the name of that love, I should not have taken the childish criminal step I had. Now, most likely, I'll never see Moscow again.

But that is not the most important thing. What's more important is my daughter, my wife and my mother. I want to ask three things of you, boys. One of them may well be too serious. Even so I beg you, in the name of our friendship, to do what I ask of you.

1) Write a letter to my wife from all of you. Explain the situation at the editorial office, explain that I'm not a criminal. In short, find words, which may in some way alleviate her grief. I'm relying on you, Danny, most of all. It will be best to give the letter to someone who is going back. It will never get there by post.

2) My little daughter is left without any means of support. Whether you can or not, you must do this, — and this is my most serious request — you must send her at the Kuibyshev address if only 300 rubles a month, as much as you can. And another thing, send it in my name. Otherwise, my wife's parents will not accept it.

3) Answer every letter you get from me. Inform those who know me that I've been transferred to a different detachment, and I'll write from there. Write the same things to my parents. But if there is no other address for me, if I cannot write, then write to them a second time, explaining what has happened. Otherwise they will go out of their mind, getting no letters from me. But if I do have an address, send me all letters without fail.

This I entrust to you, Nahum. In the letter to Bela tell her I'll be sending as much money as I can for our daughter. It's your money I mean, of course.

These are my three requests. Once again I beg you never to forget them.

Rather than live the life I see ahead of me, it would be better not to live at all. But I'll do my best. If it turns out to be pointless, then there will be a way out. In that case don't stand in judgement of me, but understand me. Remember Miller was not a bad fellow on the whole; he loved life, not just any sort of life, but our sort, the Soviet way; he wished his country happiness and always sought to help in building this happiness; he loved books and music, he hated war and became a stupid victim of war...

If I don't live to see the day of victory — and most likely I won't — I would like to believe that you will, and that some day in peacetime, you'll think of me, too. I also hope you won't fall victim to your youthful desires. In these harsh times they are not forgiven.

I'm writing you fine rose-coloured words while hell rages in my heart and at times my mind feels as if it will give way.

That, too, may happen. Again I entreat you, do what I have asked you. Do not forget me. Help me if you can. I rely on you. I embrace you all.

Your Misha

P.S. If you get to Moscow, be sure to go and see Bela.

Soon after the editorial staff was disbanded for submitting a collective report in defence of my father. All the friends were sent to different places and lost touch until the end of the war.

Each did something to help my father, but all to no avail. During the 'anti-cosmopolitan' campaign after the war, they were accused of 'defending a deserter in wartime' on top of the other charges. They visited my mother in Moscow a couple of times and even sent money for a while, but then stopped. They had problems of their own, life was not easy for them either.

St. Petersburg-Leningrad

The summer of 1954 was a special one. That summer I wrote my first story, learned to ride a bike, fell in love for the first time and first visited Leningrad. 'You're fourteen,' Mother said, 'you're a big girl now. We can go to Leningrad.' And go to Leningrad we did. Granny arranged it by writing to a distant relative of ours called Flora, who lived with her grown son Igor on Sadovaya Street. My first Leningrad impressions were of a big communal apartment, grey covers on the chairs and divans in Flora's room and curtains drawn tight to keep the light out. 'So the wallpaper doesn't fade,' our hostess explained. Short, still handsome, a hoarse voice and the invariable cigarette in her mouth, she adored and spoilt her tall, good-looking son. He was rude to her, but she worshipped him. 'There are no girls in Leningrad good enough for him. He says he'll marry one that comes up to his elbow,' Flora repeated almost every day.

Mother and I had to share a bed, sleeping head to toe for the whole fortnight. That was really all we needed, because we only spent the night at Flora's. Mother took her house slippers with her each day and put them on when her feet got tired, amidst the gold and marble of the St Petersburg palaces. I was embarrassed by this at first, expecting people to laugh, but then I got used to it.

In those two weeks we went round everything we could. Mother bought lots of guides and other books and read them to me on the way. The Grand Caprice, the Chinese Palace, the Grotto, the Colonnade, Peter the Great's boat, the Peacock clock, the 'Boy Taking out a Splinter' — all this was jumbled up in my head. The palaces and parks were not so much museums as a sleeping kingdom where I was graciously allowed to enter and examine all the details: the clothes, tea sets, paintings and clocks of bygone days. I became immersed in a different age, far more romantic and attractive than my own. But I was quite taken aback when Mother suddenly stopped me on a little hunchback bridge and said: 'Pushkin used to walk here.' I looked down and felt wobbly at the knees. Particularly because we were always economising on food so as to see more. 'You choose: one cheese sandwich and a visit to Peterhof or two sandwiches and no Peterhof,' Mother used to say when we went into a canteen. I chose one sandwich, of course, and devoured the second with my eyes.

What impressed me more than all the palaces was the house on the Moika, Pushkin's last home. I think the museum there had just opened. There were very few people there, maybe five. The guide was a young woman who took us round the rooms recounting everything as if she knew it firsthand. In Pushkin's study she told us about his last few hours, her voice trembled. I too felt a lump in my throat. I think everyone had tears in their eyes. Never since have I met a guide who relived so intensely events that happened more than a century ago.

A special feeling for that house stayed with me for many years. I longed to take my own children there. When I thought my eldest son was old enough, I rushed him off to Leningrad and took him to the house on the Moika. The tiny vestibule was packed full. We had to wait ages for the group in front to go out before we could go in. It was cramped and stuffy inside. The tired guide's voice was depressingly flat. I tried to position my son so that he could at least see and hear something, but it was no good. Moving on to the next room we found ourselves by the door which the attendant closed after us as the next group entered. I realised there would be nothing but crowds, pushing and shoving and we better escape into the fresh air. Suddenly I saw my son turn pale and his knees buckled. At that moment the door behind us flew open and a woman from the other group practically fell into the room. The crush had made her faint too. The attendant brought us some water and we sat down by the window, then made our way to the exit. When a few years later I came to Leningrad with my younger son we did not get into the house on the Moika: it was either closed for repairs or the queue was too long. But remembering how my other son had nearly fainted, I was not too sorry to miss it.

In June 1954, when Mother and I spent the 'white nights' wandering round the city, I too almost fainted at times. But this was mainly due to an excess of feelings and impressions. Everything Mother said I took absolutely literally: Pushkin walked here, the Queen of Spades lived there, Raskolnikov went across this courtyard. Our departure from Leningrad was a real tragedy for me. Fancy leaving this magic world to return to everyday life! 'Do let's stay a bit longer, just one more day,' I begged. That was the only time I was ever unfaithful to Moscow, which I always missed no matter where I was.

Muzyka — Music

The Russian word *muka* (torment) consists of the first and last syllables of the word *muzyka* (music). And this is not happenstance. For music and torment are inseparable. Is it not torment to hear a melody inside you and be unable to reproduce it because your fingers or vocal chords will not obey? This was precisely my predicament at music school.

'You are musical,' they would say to me in the same tone that an ugly girl is told she has beautiful hair or expressive eyes. 'To Larissa Miller, participant in the Best Performance of the Bach Competition and pupil of Music School No.1, Leninsky district, Moscow, for musicality' is the inscription written obliquely on the cover of Rachmaninoff's *Melodies*. What lay behind the fine sounding word 'musicality' I remember in vivid detail. Applied to me it meant that from the second bar of any piece requiring a bit of pace my fingers would refuse to obey me and begin to live an unpredictable and uncontrollable life of their own, racing ahead, barely moving, or sliding off the keys completely. Oh, how I longed to disappear, to vanish into thin air, but I was chained to the instrument like Prometheus to his rock, and had to perform, tormenting the audience, the music and myself to the bitter end. When I finally had the moral right to remove my hands from the keyboard and leave the stage, I found that my legs refused to obey me too: they shook, stumbled and would not bend at the knee. 'Make a bow, make a bow', the head teacher hissed. But how could I? Ah, music, music...

I first discovered its existence at the age of two, when we were evacuated to Kuibyshev during the war. Granny was going through my evening bath ritual. As it transpired, this procedure caused her great difficulty and was considered one of her many achievements, which she recalled many years later not without a sense of pride. And rightly so. In spite of the war, cold, hunger, and long food queues which began when it was still dark, the zinc bath brought from Moscow with its constant companion, an old brown electric stove, was set up on the table 'every evening at the appointed hour'. Granny would sponge me, pouring water over me from a jug, then wrap me in a big towel and carry me over to the springy mattress, where I would jump, frolic and chatter endlessly.

But one day, from the corner of the room or, rather, from the black loudspeaker hanging there, came a song that stilled me. 'We'll pick up our new rifles / With flags on the tips / And go off to the war / With a song on our lips...', sang a muffled, somehow receding voice, uttering these words with hisses and whistles that made them even more enigmatic. For some reason I imagined a line of children crouching (so the enemy would not see them), holding rifles and wearing peaked helmets with red stars on them marching along to this song. As I listened to this dying voice, shivers ran down my spine. The song had brought something new and frightening into the room, where the red coil of the electric fire still shone cosily and there was a habitual smell of freshly scrubbed floors.

This moment marked the beginning of my long, varied and highly complex relationship with music. One musical passion followed another, each like an acute form of illness. I remember glancing one day at the score of *Evgeny Onegin*, which I usually sat on when I was practising, and without knowing why picking out the overture with one hand. This was so absorbing, that I completely forgot about my set pieces, entranced by the restrained and sorrowful sighs at the end of each phrase.

But if *Evgeny Onegin* excited the primary school pupil, it was the *Nightingale Tango* that thrilled the adolescent. The violins there, how they rippled, sighed and sobbed, and how short-lived my love of them proved to be. It died on that day in March when some friends of Mother's and mine came to my birthday: the writer Uncle Alyosha and the music critic Aunt Liza. No sooner had they crossed the threshold of our room, than I dragged them over to the gramophone and put on the record, by now rather scratchy from my excessive passion for it. When the violins began to sob, I looked at our friends expecting to see emotion and tears in their eyes. But instead of tears and emotion I found astonished glances and derisive smiles. When the last strains had died away, Uncle Alyosha began drumming his fingers on the table in silence, while Aunt Liza asked in a voice full of compassion: 'Do you really like that?', to which I replied treacherously and unexpectedly for myself 'I don't know'. The spell was broken.

Love and perfidy, music and infidelity are nearly always inseparable. How many there have been in my life — favourite records played to death, ruined by my insatiable passion and then abandoned for many years. At different times in my life I played to death Schumann's *Carnival*, Beethoven's sonatas, Bach's *Brandenburg Concertos*, Chopin's piano concertos, and his sonata in A-flat with its impetuous opening, full of melancholy and confusion, that almost drove me crazy. It followed me from dawn to dusk, echoing inside me whatever I was doing, but as soon as I put the record on, it was all over in a few seconds, leaving me longing for the beginning again.

One day Mother brought two large and splendid foreign records. The glossy sleeve of one sported the American flag, a sheet of music, an army service cap and a pince-nez with the words 'A TRIBUTE TO GLENN MILLER'. The other was Gershwin's *Porgy and Bess*. A new era began in my life — the era of jazz. Alongside records of Gershwin and Miller appeared Ella Fitzgerald, Louis Armstrong, Duke Ellington, and Frank Sinatra. I did not so much listen as dance to all this, swaying and turning, inventing all sorts of strange movements in my endless desire to merge with the music, become part of it and albeit for a short time lose the tormenting sense of unrequited love for it.

There was a time when I actually believed that music really could belong to me and be played for me alone. The person who made me believe this was my blond-haired, blue-eyed boyfriend, who played the piano exquisitely and dedicated each note to me.

'What do you see in her?' I read in his mother's eyes when I was invited home. 'What did I see in her?' I read in his eyes the next day. We went on meeting and he still played me Liszt's 'Liebestraum', Schumann's 'Dedication' and other pieces from Van Cliburn's repertoire which he adored in that unforgettable year of 1958. But now each note told me 'It's not for you, not yours.'

'For you, for you, for you,' I was to hear many years later from other lips. Again someone tried to give me what cannot be possessed: love and music. The snow on the roof was melting and the steady drip reminded me of Brahms' Intermezzo, a great favourite of mine then. Each note, as solitary as a drop falling from the roof, traversed its fatal path and vanished into space. It was drawn to the sinful earth, as if someone had promised that only by passing through all the earthly circuits and undergoing a series of painful transformations could it acquire new life and rise to new heights. Everything is possible in music: a reprise enables you to return the past, a fermata to stop the moment, and the keyboard to acquire stability. Music is an attempt to create heaven on earth (here they are, the keys to heaven on a sheet of music), an attempt to entreat fate, to build bridges over the abyss, to combine the uncombinable. A desperate and hopeless attempt. No wonder one of Schnittke's most enchanting melodies suddenly falls apart, disintegrates and turns into something ugly and shapeless, as if mocking its own beauty. Music is a werewolf that can take on an angelic or diabolical guise. Music is a great temptation, a tower of Babel, a staircase that constantly strives for the heavens, yet may collapse at any moment. And happiness is simply a chance of not perishing beneath the rubble.

> *Music, music, my joy and torment,*
> *Ancient secret of the birth of sound*
> *Which exists in space and roams around,*
> *Tormenting my soul and healing it too.*

Music, music, forte and piano -
You are both balsam and open wound
Divine providence and devilish guile,
Music, music, piano and forte.

Flitting and Gliding

She used to come to use the phone. Or, to be more precise, not come, but glide down from the top floor where she lived. There would be three quick rings at the door, and the semi-dark corridor of our communal apartment filled with the special, subtle aroma that followed her, like a train, into our room where the phone stood on Mother's desk. She perched right on the edge of the chair, pulling her dressing gown more closely around her, and dialled the number she needed. I was always taken out of the room while she was talking. Probably because I gaped at her all the while. To me she was an ethereal creature, weightless and incorporeal. Slender and lithe, her pale, transparent face covered with a thin layer of cream, her voice low and melodic, she never got in the way and took up very little room, yet somehow filled the space around her. And not only filled, but transformed it, turning our ordinary, somewhat squalid accommodation into a mysterious place from another world.

After making a few calls and whispering to Mother, she vanished noiselessly, leaving the tiny whiff of her perfume for us to remember her by. Sometimes when I came back from a walk and sniffed, I was annoyed to find that Ksyusha, as she was called affectionately in our family, had been, or rather flitted in while I was out. It was only later that I discovered she was an actress by the name of Constancia Royek. I never managed to see her on the stage, but the role she played in my life, without actually realising it, was unique: it aroused in me the passionate urge to be ethereal, sylph-like, and learn to walk without touching the ground. No sooner had she gone out of the door, than I tried to cross the room on tiptoe. But stopped in horror at the sight of my reflection in the mirror.

Goodness me, what a sight! Shoulders hunched up and toes turned in. Stopping in front of the mirror, I made a desperate attempt to put my heels together and keep my toes apart, but for some reason this made my shoulders hunch up and the palms of my hands turn out. What could I do if I had inherited flat feet from both parents, plus pigeon toes from my father? All the same, I did not give up hope. Putting on something white and wispy, I tried to flit round the Christmas tree like a snowflake. At a summer camp concert I played the part of a stork and stalked round the lawn, picking my feet up high. But no matter how hard I tried, my stork had pigeon toes, a fact stubbornly borne out by the numerous photographs.

Notwithstanding I continued to wait and hope. What for? Well, that Ksyusha would reappear and reveal at least part of the secret of her ethereality. And she did appear now and then. Under her fingers even the lock on the door did not give its usual raucous screech, but sang sweetly, to announce her miraculous coming.

Why she came to use our phone, when all the other communal apartments (hers included) had one, I do not know. Perhaps because she did not always want to speak in front of the neighbours, and in our apartment, apart from the communal telephone in the corridor, there was one in our room (a privilege granted to Mother when she started working on the radio). Actually I was not a bit concerned about these prosaic details. What really interested me was the strange fact that I never saw Ksyusha on the stairs or in the yard, although I often saw her handsome, dark-haired husband, the well-known Bolshoi Theatre dancer Yuri Gofman, walking with his professional springy step across the yard, a suitcase in his hand. He was completely real to me, but she, who appeared now and then in our dark flat on the ground floor, remained a miraculous mirage that one day disappeared forever.

Actually it was we who disappeared when we moved. One spring day in the school entrance hall I was surprised to see a petite young woman in a short summer dress gliding over the tiled floor as if it were a skating rink. 'Volskaya, Volskaya,' came the whispers from all sides. 'Who's Volskaya?' I asked my classmate. 'Don't you know? She's an actress at the operetta and lives in your block. Her daughter goes to our school.'

A few days later I looked out of the window and saw Volskaya again, walking along our street with her light dancing step. I watched until she turned the corner.

Incredible. So here too was a creature in the same block who tormented me with her ethereal weightlessness. Unlike Ksyusha there was nothing ghostlike about Volskaya. You could see her shaking rugs deftly and cheerfully in the yard and almost dancing as she carried out the garbage, 'down the stairs, two steps at a time, she flew like dizzy lightning ...' into the ordinary world where she knew how to live, flitting and gliding.

There was nothing I wanted more than to learn to dance. I went on at Mother's dressmaker, who had once been in the corps de ballet, and made her teach me the ballet positions. Then I would turn on the radio and twirl round to the music until I dropped. But each day I had to listen to my dearly beloved Grandfather grumbling: 'Don't be so pigeon-toed, dear. Don't clatter about. Lift up your legs.' Oh, dear, why hadn't I inherited Grandfather's light step? To each his own. It was my sad fate. No, I must do something about it. I listened to my inner voice that told me to fight the force of gravity.

Eventually, when I already had a small son, the impossible happened: I found a place where I learnt to be weightless. No, it wasn't the astronauts' training centre, but a school gym on Tsvetnoy Boulevard, where twice a week an event took place that had elements of an angels' congregation, a witches' sabbath and the rites of some strange sect, but was actually Alexeyeva's Gym Studio. Alexeyeva's because it had originally been set up and run by the dancer Ludmila Alexeyeva. By the time I crossed the threshold of the gym, where members of the female sex were whirling, flitting and gliding about, Alexeyeva was no more. She had died in 1964 of cancer. I was told that even when she was ill she continued to come regularly to the school, climbing up to the fifth floor and giving the lessons half lying down. In the last year of her life she tried to revive an etude she composed before the war on a theme from Gluck's *Orpheus and Eurydice.*

By the time I joined the group in 1969 the classes were conducted by Alexeyeva's pupils. The studio's veteran pianist sat at the grand piano playing all sorts of music, from Bach to old foxtrots. And Gluck's divine music to which Eurydice's friends lament her death, while the Furies refuse to let Orpheus into the underworld. Eurydice herself flitted round the hall as if in her sleep.

I was ready to join all the existing groups, including the children's, where I was invited to help the teacher. And so it was that performing the 'Stork' together with the children, I again found myself, as I had some twenty years before, walking on tiptoe and lifting my knees up high. Do I turn my toes in? I expect so. But I imagine that I do not. I imagine myself running gracefully, jumping high and hovering over the floor for a moment. 'You're a perfect sylph,' Alexeyeva's oldest student told me one day. A sylph, as you know, is a spirit of the air. Was this not what my heart craved?

> *I fly, I glide tirelessly*
> *Along the golden corridor.*
> *My lodestar at this time*
> *The thread of an autumnal web*
> *Or falling leaves.*
> *And I live as if chance is*
> *Powerless over my fate.*

If I hadn't found this studio and experienced the wonderful sense of flying, I would never have been able to write these lines and many more besides.

> *Everything hangs in the air.*
> *The foundation is not real.*
> *The bird flaps its wing,*

The rain drizzles.
All is in the air: the window
The staircase, the roof,
They talk, and breathe,
And sleep, when it is dark,
And get up again with the dawn.
And at dawn, barefoot,
I circle and hover
Between earth and heaven.

A few years ago, talking to an actress I know, I mentioned the name of Constancia Royek. 'Ksyusha?' she repeated, then added with a sigh: 'Poor Ksyusha. She had to leave the stage a long time ago: she was suffering from severe nervous depression. Spent ages in hospital, but it didn't help.'

Sic transit... Thus even those who do not seem to touch the earth are dragged down in the end. Such is the force of gravity, the pull of the earth, the earthly burden.

The Black Sea

We took large suitcases with us travelling to the Black Sea on our summer vacations. They were so full that stepfather had to kneel on top of them, while Mother bit her lip trying to fasten them. At the station we got a porter and, telling me not to lag behind, they almost ran after him along the platform, bumping into people with the bags there was no room for on the trolley.

To save money we travelled in a third-class sleeper. When we stopped by our carriage, where a crowd was waiting to be let in, I glanced enviously at the neighbouring wagon-lit, which people were happily boarding without a wait.

The journey south was a long one, but I liked trains, lying on my stomach on the top bunk and looking out of the open window with the wind blowing in and making my eyes water. After a while, of course, you got a tickle in your throat, soot in your nose and specks of grit in your eyes. Yet the whole of the first day I lay on the top bunk, too lazy to get down when they brought tea. Although drinking tea on a train has a special fascination. When the top bunk lost its novelty, food became the main attraction. 'Go and see if they're bringing the tea,' they told me. And I would happily trot up to the giant samovar and stroke it to see whether the attendant was heating the water and getting the glasses ready, jingling the spoons and laying out enticing lumps of sugar in paper wrappings. And if she was, out came the boiled eggs, the matchbox with salt, the penknife, cold chicken legs, cucumbers and tomatoes — the usual train journey fare, which gave me the kind of wolfish appetite I never had at home. Mother knew this and did her best to feed me up during the journey.

There was one more attraction — the goods on sale at the different stops, more and more tempting the further south you got: hot potatoes on big cabbage leaves, crunchy salted cucumbers with sprigs of dill stuck to them, cold yoghurt, home-baked flat bread, and further south — apples, plums and honeydew melons. Right in their striped pyjamas and long housecoats travellers hopped out of the train and made their way, slippers flapping and heels tapping, to the buckets, baskets and sacks. Purses snapped, voices were raised excitedly and people rushed up and down the platform until, finally, the steam engine whistled, the flag waved and off we went again. The passengers disappeared into their compartments and the feasting began. Our neighbour saw a young lad walking along the platform with some melons, pushed the money out of the window and shouted: 'Hey, lad! One melon! For three rubles!' Taking the three-rouble note, the young man held up a melon, but the train started to move and the melon slowly receded. Our neighbour stretched out his hand and the boy stretched out the melon, but the train gathered speed. We lamented the lost melon until the next stop, at which we bought another one and ate it all together. Between eating and sleeping we used to play whispers, fool, black and white, and hangman — when you have to guess the letters in a word before you get drawn on the gallows. One leg, two legs, right arm, left arm, cucumber body, thin neck, round head with eyes, nose, mouth and ears. Not long to go, and you still haven't found the right letters. All the way I made Mother hang me, and when she got tired of it, I persuaded our neighbours. The only bad things about the train were the heat and the dirt. The whole carriage smelt of the toilet. This smell even survived our arrival.

The place we always went to was Gagry. Mysterious Gagry, where they always put on the same scratchy record in the summer cinema at the beginning of each show, and the needle used to get stuck. 'The weary sun so g-g-gently, g-g-gently, g-g-gently...' rang out over the village. Our landlady Vera Nikolayevna, an elderly woman with short hair, a shiny bracelet on her thin wrist and heavy earrings, was always smiling, her face shiny with face cream. They said she was from Leningrad and had moved to Gagry many years ago with her professor husband because of his health. When her husband died, she married a huge, fat Georgian whose surname was Kiberia and who adored Rossini's *The Barber of Seville*. Everybody who rented a room from them brought him records of this opera. When Kiberia was at home he usually sat in the round summerhouse overgrown with wild vines where he and Vera Nikolayevna lived in summer, listening to his Rossini: 'Figaro, Figaro, bravo, bravissimo...'. One day Vera Nikolayevna sent me to get some cigarettes from him. Pulling aside the coloured curtains hanging at the door, I saw heavy, hairy Kiberia in blue shorts and a pale blue vest sitting by the gramophone, eyes half-closed, singing in time with the record, an expression of rapture on his face. I took the cigarettes from the table quietly and left.

How picturesque Gagry was with all the sheds, verandas, and summerhouses, packed to overflowing with holidaymakers. Some people slept on camp beds or beach mats under banana trees or some fragrant shrub, paying a mere fifty kopecks a day. Mother's cousin, who spent a whole month sleeping outside, woke up one night to find his face being licked by a huge stray dog. He turned over onto his other side, leaving the dog the back of his neck, and went to sleep again. The place was on a hill, and we had to climb up there in the heat several times a day: from the beach, from the local market or the post office. When we arrived we felt like going back again for a dip in the sea. But instead we flopped down on the bed and lay there until we'd cooled down.

Once a week Mother woke me up early before it got hot

and we hurried to the bus which had to be taken by storm. Squeezed in on all sides, we endured until the last stop. 'Market!' shouted the driver and out tumbled the perspiring passengers. The market was abuzz with sounds and the colourful stalls quite dazzling. Moving from stall to stall, Mother didn't simply make purchases, but performed a kind of ritual: fingering, tasting, rejecting, hesitating, going away only to come back again. Now and then I lost her and ran round looking for her in a panic. 'Hold this bag,' she would say. 'Watch what you're doing. Hold it properly. Can't you see it's spilling.' I gradually turned stupid from the heat, the crowd, the strangeness of everything and the general uproar. Praising their wares, Caucasians would grab us by the arm. One even rushed out from behind his stall and pulled me over to give me an apple the size of a melon.

By the entrance to the market squatted the sellers of wine and cheese. The pale damp discs of cheese lay on snow-white pieces of cloth. They would pour you a mug of wine to taste from a huge bottle. 'Drink it up, dear, don't be afraid and give your daughter some. It's pure grapes.' The wine was sweet and pungent. After a gulp or two, I couldn't stop myself and drank it all down. A cheese seller looked at me with a smile and handed me a piece of *sulguni cheese*. 'Here, have a bite of cheese. It's as young as you are.'

After the market we always dropped in to see Isachok, who smoked and sold mackerel he'd caught. I have only a vague memory of the picturesque courtyard smelling of smoked fish and nets hanging up to dry, there were neat strips of glass laid out all over the place that Isachok used for smoking the fish. Isachok himself, a swarthy convivial middle-aged man with curly black hair always greeted us in a long apron and, after supplying us with fish, accompanied us to the gate, assuring us that we would lick our fingers and swallow our tongue, as he put it.

After my stepfather appeared, which was in 1951, we went to Gagry every summer. But for some reason I remember the summer of 1954 best of all, when I wore a long pinafore of printed cotton in the daytime and a silk dress with frills instead of sleeves in the evening, when passers-by turned round to look at me, and hot-blooded Caucasians leaned out of their cars to shout something and wave their arms. One day, when I was waiting for Mother by the post office, a box fell at my feet and a pair of bright earrings rolled out of it. Looking up I saw a young man sitting on a first floor windowsill, pressing his hand to his heart and smiling.

That summer I had very long eyelashes, very dark eyebrows and very wavy hair. It was my second flowering. My last flowering was in the Kazakh steppe, in 1958, and my first in early childhood when, according to Granny, I had such rosy cheeks that they didn't look real and you wanted to touch them.

In 1954 there was a whole gaggle of girls about my age living in Vera Nikolayevna's many sheds and shacks.. We used to flock down to the beach together with two black inflatable tires. Wading out a bit, we would stretch out on the tire and sing at the top of our voices: 'Twelve little black boys swimming in the sea / Twelve little black boys splashing merrily / Then one got drowned / And buried in the ground / So there were / Eleven little black boys...' we shouted and, if we had the energy we would start again from the beginning.

There was a very complicated nightlife going on. I would

sometimes be woken by footsteps, giggles and squeals. By morning all was quiet, and when Mother and I went down to the sea everyone was fast asleep. Not everyone, of course. The 'righteous' ones, like our family, got up early and did the usual holiday things: making breakfast, going to the market or hurrying to get their full share of morning sun. One day we heard that a 'sinner' had appeared among the 'righteous', sixteen-year-old Asya, who started going off to the dancing rink at night and came back accompanied by a local boy with a moustache. One morning I saw Asya's mother, very upset and weeping, talking to Vera Nikolayevna in a choking voice: 'I went out to make Asya go to bed, and he walked up to me and said "mother". I nearly fainted. What could "mother" mean? What's that little tart been up to?' I deliberately spent a long time sweeping up in the kitchen so as to hear more. Fancy that, Asya, who had sunbathed on the tire with me, also had a mysterious nightlife. And the word 'mother' that had also become a mystery... Asya was soon packed off home to Kaluga, and our ranks grew thinner. Of those who remained I liked Natasha and her grandfather, a professor of medicine from Tula. I don't know which of them I liked best.

Vera Nikolayevna's main house was full of very old things brought from Leningrad years ago: armchairs, lamps and books. In the middle of the dark drawing room stood an out-of-tune grand piano with music on it. All this must have belonged to her first husband. One day, when I was looking through the music, Natasha's grandfather came in. 'Well, what have you found there?' he asked. 'Some old music.' 'Ah, that's Gounod's *Faust.* Adapted for piano. Can you play?' 'It depends what,' I said, leafing through it until I came to Siebel's aria. 'I could play this.' After a few false starts I played it quite nicely. Natasha's grandfather stood behind me singing: 'Tell her, my flowers...' He sang in a funny high-pitched voice, but perfectly in tune. We enjoyed music-making so much that we started coming to the room each day and even acquired an audience. But one day it had to be called off. I got a high temperature. As she hurried to the chemist's Mother asked Natasha's grandfather to go and see me. He came into the room and sat down on the edge of the bed. After touching my forehead and asking me to show him my throat, he began to stroke my shoulders and arms gingerly with his hand. 'Would you like me to tickle your feet?' he asked. 'What for?' I said in surprise, not knowing what to make of this strange fondling and feeling rather uncomfortable. 'If you're afraid of being tickled, that means you're amorous.' 'Stop it.' He ran his hand along my leg. 'You've got musical toes.' At that moment Mother came back. Natasha's grandfather removed his hand and got up. 'She got too hot,' he said. 'She'll be alright.' Unable to explain what had happened, I began to avoid him.

Then life changed abruptly. Two students appeared in the room next to ours. I had heard about them from slim, big-eyed Stella who had come to stay at Vera Nikolayevna's with her friend Rimma before we arrived. 'When my boyfriend comes, I'll wear this dress,' Stella kept saying. 'When my boyfriend comes, we'll go to a restaurant. When my boyfriend comes...' And now the boyfriend had come. His name was Natan. I saw him when I came back from the beach one afternoon. He had dark hair and dark eyes. 'Black prince,' I thought. Why 'prince' — I don't know. From the moment he appeared I no longer wanted to have an afternoon nap, but to sit on our shared veranda and write the story I had started that spring.

I went out onto the veranda with my notebook, pencil and rubber, sat down at the round table and began staring into the distance, at the sea. Alas, Natan did not often find me in this pose. He lived that strange nightlife, which passed me by, and his regime did not coincide with mine. But one day he was at home and appeared on the terrace at the very moment when inspiration came to me. 'What are you writing?' he asked. 'A story,' I replied, continuing to write. 'A story?' he repeated in surprise. I shrugged my shoulders, which was meant to say: 'What's so special about that. I do it all the time.' 'What's it about?' 'A children's home and a family,' I replied using the rubber. 'A children's home?' Natan was even more surprised. I was on top of the world. So far everything was going splendidly: his surprise and my composure, his admiration and my modesty. But when I finally dared to look up, I saw he could hardly contain his laughter. 'He's laughing at me,' I thought in horror. 'All this time he's been laughing at me.' I got up to leave. 'Read it to me,' Natan asked. 'No,' I said abruptly and left the room.

I still went down to the sea in the mornings, lazed on the lilo with the girls, went to the market with Mother and to the cinema with her too, but at the same time I led another life, invisible to the outside world. Going to sleep, I would listen to the voices behind the wall. Sunbathing on the beach, I would gaze at the point where the 'black prince' was sitting in the company of Stella and Rimma. Returning from the market I would glance at the neighbouring door. Although I hardly ever saw him, I managed to study his habits: I knew how he laughed, swam and walked. Sometimes I unexpectedly found his black eyes gazing at me attentively and this sent my temperature up. One day, coming back from the sea, I saw a lock on the next door. Surely he hadn't gone away! It turned out that the four of them, Natan and his friend, Stella and Rimma had gone to the nearby city of Sukhumi for a few days. Time stopped. How could I live until my 'black prince' returned? The cinema, the park and the beach all bored me to tears. What did a few days mean? Five? Seven? Ten? Then suddenly the lock disappeared. The door opened slightly, and inside was Natan. 'So you're still here. I was afraid you might leave while we were away without reading me your story.' 'Afraid!' He had said 'afraid'. 'I'll read it if you like,' I blurted out and, breathless from my daring, I went to fetch my notebook. I had to hurry. I could only read it if Mother wasn't there. When she was, I seemed to become wooden. I got the notebook, sat down on the wicker table (probably thinking that this made me look more grown-up and relaxed) and began to read. When I finished, Natan clapped. 'Well, how about that. Just like Tolstoy. I want to show off too. Will you come and watch me play volleyball? It's not far. There's a coach to take us.' 'What? On my own?' I didn't know what to say. 'Bring your parents if you like.'

Next day we set off along a narrow shady road. Branches kept coming through the open windows of the coach, and Natan, who was sitting in front of us by the window, kept pushing them away. The match was on the volleyball court at some holiday home. It was between two amateur teams. I didn't know the rules of the game, but quietly swooned as I watched Natan hit the ball, sometimes almost falling to the ground, sometimes leaping right up. I felt like a beautiful lady watching her knight at a tournament: all these leaps and falls were in my honour.

On the way back Mother asked Natan to help me with square roots. It was September, school had already begun and we were not planning to get back to Moscow until the fourteenth. 'Please help her. She's no good at maths,' Mother explained. 'But she writes like Tolstoy,' Natan laughed. After that he helped me with square roots each morning. He even set me some homework, which I used to start straightaway after the lesson. Square roots are perhaps the only bit of maths that I have ever learnt.

Then it was time to leave. Leaving Gagry was no easy matter. The train stopped for one minute only to let a big crowd of people get on. I always dreaded that moment. But this time I was thinking about something else: where was Natan? Where had he gone? I was oblivious to all around me. Someone pushed some bags into my hands and told me to go somewhere. I did as I was told, stopped and answered, but all the time I was thinking: where is Natan? Eventually the train appeared. Everyone grabbed their luggage and rushed to the carriages. We did the same. Suitcases, packages and bags bobbed overhead, children cried, women squealed, men swore. And at this moment HIS face appeared in the crowd. 'That box of fruit over there is ours,' stepfather shouted to him. Natan picked up the box and joined us. He took Mother's bags and passed them to stepfather. Then he helped me and Mother squeeze onto the train, waved and disappeared.

After a moment's elation, my spirits dropped. That was it, I would never see him again. We settled down in the carriage, putting the luggage away, and just as we were getting our breath back, there was Natan in the doorway. 'What are you doing here?' said Mother in surprise. 'Oh, I'm travelling on the same train, only third-class. 'Why? Where are your friends?' 'They stayed on, but I'd had enough. So I went and bought a ticket today.' He looked at me and smiled. 'It's because of me, because of me,' my head sang. 'Have some tea with us,' Mother said. 'I'd have to get settled now, but I'll come by later.'

The carriage was fast asleep when he came. I was lying on the top bunk with my head by the door so as not to miss him. He came up to me and said: 'Want to learn how to read my name? It's got a secret.' He took an indelible pencil out of his pocket, spat on it, and wrote 'Natan' on my palm. 'Don't wash your hand and read my name backwards and forwards every morning.' This discovery amazed me. 'You know, I really like you,' Natan said quietly, pulling my plait gently. 'Even Stella got jealous and went home early. Did you know that?' I didn't. Everything he said seemed so incredible that I couldn't take it in. 'Can we meet in Moscow? Go to the theatre? Or the cinema?' asked Natan, still fingering my plait. I thought I was dreaming. He was in his last year at college, while I was in the eighth year at school. He was twenty-one and I was fourteen. Yet here he was standing next to me saying these unbelievable things. On the next bunk a fat man snored away, while further down a child sniffled, and someone was talking in their sleep. 'You'd better get some sleep. I'll come tomorrow.' The black prince set off down the corridor, stepping round someone's feet, avoiding bags and almost tripping over a pair of shoes.

As soon as I got back to Moscow he rang and came round. I sat at the table telling him about my class that now contained such exotic creatures as boys. (It was the first year of co-education). Compared with the black prince all our boys seemed small and silly. Natan and I had tea and I went with him to the metro. I was wearing my school uniform and he was in a black suit and green velour hat. I kept looking round hoping to meet someone from my class. That evening I told Mother about Natan. She showered me with questions, wanting to know everything. I hesitated, then told her that when I jumped up from the table, he caught hold of me, held me for a moment in the air, then somehow reluctantly let me go. When Natan rang again, Mother answered and asked him not to come for a while. 'She's very busy,' she said. 'She has music school on top of the regular school.' He asked to talk to me, and I repeated the same thing in a dull voice. 'Is that your last word?' he asked grimly. I hung up, afraid of bursting into tears. 'He'll be back,' said Mother, watching my face carefully. And he was.

***

They made me a white dress for my sixteenth birthday. When I put it on a year later for the school-leaving ball, the waist was in the wrong place and the skirt was too short. All this matched my inner state. I always detested school get-togethers and hardly ever went to them. But how could I get out of going to the school-leaving ball? Nobody would have understood at school or at home. Mother spent the whole day in a sentimental mood and was planning to go with me. But I dissuaded her and set off on my own. There were crowds of town boys by the entrance, who were turned away by attendants with red bands on their sleeves. After edging my way past some tipsy young men as inconspicuously as possible, I went into the cloakroom. There I found bevies of Snow Whites flitting across the tiled floor. They had such extravagant hair-dos, excited faces and unnatural high laughs that I hardly recognised them. The boys were dressed in their Sunday best and behaved with a sober gravity. I felt out of place, at a loss who to latch on to. During the official ceremony in the school hall it was so stuffy that I kept glancing longingly at the door, quite out of reach, alas. The medals and certificates of merit were duly distributed. I was not among the recipients. The only time I ever had all top marks was in the fifth form.

After the speeches and awards everyone crowded into the hall for food and music. I nibbled an apple, ate a cake and washed it down with lemonade. Then the worst part came, the dancing. 'Perhaps I could slip away now?' I thought. But what would I say to Mother when she asked why I was home so early? So I went back into the hall, which had now been aired and the chairs removed. I latched on to a group of excited classmates, but did not manage to join in the conversation, interrupted by explosive giggles. The more active ones were already dancing. I was out of it on all counts: no medals, no certificates, no boyfriend, no girlfriends.

Then suddenly Mikhas, the physics teacher, appeared before me — thin and tall, with a mop of fair hair. He usually wore the military uniform he had sported since the war. But tonight he was in a suit and tie. Gazing into my eyes with a meaningful smile, he took my hand and led me away from the giggling girls. Choosing a secluded spot, he leaned over and began talking. I was hardly listening, aware only that everyone was looking at us. There was the maths teacher glancing in our direction and whispering something to the literature teacher: the gym teacher had just turned round; some girls from the parallel class were running past us, giggling; and the boys were filing past with smirks. Breathing wine fumes into my face, Mikhas talked and talked. He said that I must understand him, that for a long time he had ..., that it was very important to him... Then he started coughing and pulled out the spray he always carried with him. When he got his breath back, he grabbed my hand and started running his thumb along the edge of my fingernails. It set my teeth on edge and made me feel quite sick. But what could I do? He was a teacher, and I just a pupil, what is more, a pupil who didn't understand the first thing about physics. 'Let's go to my study. It's too noisy here,' he said and began pulling me after him. I couldn't think what to do. Suddenly a group of boys rushed past us. 'We're off to Red Square. Come with us!' And unexpectedly for myself, I broke free and ran after them. 'Where are you going?' Mikhas's voice followed me. 'To Red Square', I shouted, racing down the stairs. Outside I stopped and caught my breath. The sky was low and dark, heralding the storm that broke as soon as I reached home.

Mother was still awake. Waiting up for me, of course, on such an unforgettable day. 'Come on, lass, tell us all about it.' 'Tell you what?' 'Everything in order, of course.' 'Well, first there was the official part, then the dancing.' 'But why did you come back so soon?' Mother stared into my eyes anxiously. 'Weren't you going to Red Square?' 'Yes, but then the storm started.' Lightning flashed through the window. It was just like one of those films: a heavy summer shower, the school ball, the white dress and the declaration of love. I got undressed and climbed into bed, but could not sleep. An old rhyme kept going round in my head that we used to sing in one of our childhood games: 'Black and white you must not take. Yes and no you must not say. Will you go to the ball?' 'No,' I shouted the forbidden word in my head. 'No, no, no. Never, not for anything in the world.'

Virgin Lands

(In the late fifties and sixties, as part of their Communist education, all college students were supposed to spend their summer vacations working on various construction projects or in agriculture, usually in the 'virgin lands' in Kazakhstan, Siberia and the Urals. The program for opening up 'virgin lands' was Khruschev's pet project.)

At seventeen for some reason I stopped sleeping. I lay awake all night, eyes wide open, and towards morning drifted into a kind of semi-oblivion in which I could hear everything that was going on outside or next-door, but could not move. There was our old clock on the sideboard hissing and clanging every fifteen minutes. These familiar sounds became a detestable and obtrusive background to my chronic insomnia. 'Hsss ding-dong, hsss ding-dong, can't sleep all night long,' they mocked.

Mother took me to a Moscow 'luminary', an old doctor who lived off the Arbat. The spacious study looked more like an antique shop with strangely shaped vases, thick carpets, a table lamp entwined with porcelain grapes on the desk, an ink-pot in the shape of a lion's paw under it and some elegant bronze fingers holding a pad of prescription slips. But what really caught my eye were the clocks: grandfather clocks, wall clocks, table clocks, with weights, pendulums and a cuckoo, they ticked away remorselessly, emitting various sounds, from high and melodic to low and dissonant. After so many sleepless nights spent under the hissing and ding-donging of our clock at home, to come for help to a place with nothing but the ticking and chiming of clocks of all shapes and sizes, did not augur well.

The 'luminary' entered soundlessly and invited me to sit closer to the table. Then this tiny bald person, smiling sweetly, began inquiring whether my insomnia was not perhaps the result of unrequited love. Having been persuaded that it was not, he lost interest and, taking a clean sheet from the pad, prescribed luminal. Which is what Mother took when she could not sleep. I was to take it half an hour before going to bed, and then go for a walk. After the luminal walk I came home exhausted, limp and sleepy, flopped into bed and slept for a short while, then woke up to the sound of 'Hsss ding-dong, hsss ding-dong, can't sleep all night long.'

Seeing that luminal was not the answer, Mother turned for help to Granny who had a solution for everything. She started making the journey each evening from Lefortovo where she lived then to Paveletskaya, where we lived, in order to prove to me by her personal example that there was nothing easier than going to sleep. Now the hissing and chiming was compounded by her energetic snores. Waking up in the morning she would turn to me and, at the sight of my miserable face, exclaim: 'Surely you haven't been awake all night!' Changing her tactics, she then decided to stay awake herself for a while and tell me stories or read to me. But gradually her voice faded away, becoming unintelligible, as she fell asleep. After a month she gave up. That is, she went on phoning Mother to get the latest bulletin from the front, but stopped staying the night.

Of all the measures to save me, and there were quite a few, I remember only one: the move from the large room with a communicating door to a quieter and smaller room, where I was facing the window through which I could see a street lamp that never went out swinging in the wind. In winter snowflakes danced round it. Now that the clock and I were in separate rooms its chimes were muffled which, strangely enough, was a source of additional torment to me. Now I had to strain hard so as, God forbid, not to miss the next set of mocking hisses. This tired me out so much that I lapsed into a semi-comatose state, and thanks to it, most probably, I survived.

In the end it was work that saved me, the very kind that created man from ape. In my eighteenth year I was sent to the 'virgin lands'. To the Kazakh steppes with their wormwood, endless sky, stars, elevators and grain, grain, grain. If I dreamed of anything then it was the streams of grain that I scooped up with a spade from the bottom of a lorry, and shook out of my rubber boots, but which went on and on, threatening to engulf and crush me. My sleep was deep, but short. Short because there was little time to sleep: I was either out working or out walking. But as soon as I reached my mattress on the floor I went out like a light. Thanks to Work! Thanks to the steppe air! And thanks to those walks under the moon.

Yet it was thanks to insomnia that I heard the passage of

time at that tender age, when most young people have no idea of it. Heard it moving, relentlessly, inexorably. And not only heard, but even entered into a complex, purely personal relationship with it: time was teasing me, trying to frighten me, make me despair. It became my nightmare, delirium, the only vigilant witness of my insomnia, and by an irony of fate, was personified by the good old clock with its figure of a woman reading. The clock that had always been a symbol of peace and quiet in my childhood. Now dumb and blind after an unsuccessful repair, it still lives in my home, quite unaware of the complex part it played in my life.

Although I recovered from my insomnia, I have never got rid of the disease it gave me. I don't know what it is called. Perhaps time mania, chronic chronomania. The long nights spent under the clock's ticking and chiming were not in vain. Time hypnotised me once and for all, enthralled me, taught me to try and catch its every sigh and whisper. When at the beginning of the sixties I began to write poetry one of my first efforts was about time.

Stop for a moment, time, don't go.
Stand with me by the lazy flow
Of life's river deep and slow.
Which sometimes seems to have no end,
In spite of the stubborn fact, my friend.
On this quiet bank let me see
That all is not too late for me
That I can still do what I will,
And that for me time can stand still.

Before letting her weedy eighteen-year-old go off to the 'virgin lands', after my first year at the Foreign Languages Institute, Mother decided I needed fattening up and rushed off to buy tickets to the heavenly spa of Palanga in Lithuania. One night on the train and there we were in heaven, a small seaside resort on the Baltic coast. The language we could hear everywhere was certainly not Russian. 'Is it Lithuanian?' 'Must be,' Mother replied. But it was not just Lithuanian. I recognised the familiar intonations, but could not understand the words. Yiddish. Of course, it was Yiddish, the language Granny and Grandfather used when they didn't want me to know what they were talking about. Yiddish and Lithuanian were spoken more often here than Russian. Hardly anyone in Russia had heard about Palanga in those days. We rented a room from an elderly Lithuanian woman who spoke very little Russian and hurried down to the sea. There was a yellow sandy beach. 'Dunes,' said Mother. The sea was very calm with hardly a soul in it. I got undressed and stepped into the water. It was icy cold and the bottom was sandy. I walked out for about a mile but it was still only ankle-deep, I lay on the water trying to swim with my knees scraping the bottom. Used to the Black Sea, I did not enjoy such swimming at all. But you could laze in the dunes and go for long walks in the huge leafy park. Early in the morning Mother went off hunting for food, bringing back her spoils: fresh cheeses and all sorts of cream, yoghurt and milk in bottles and boxes of different shapes and sizes. Later in the Kazakh steppes I often remembered Palanga's assorted milk products.

'NO MOANING' said a notice in big letters on our van.

The goods train waiting for us seemed endless. Mother and Natan were seeing me off. Natan was carrying my rucksack with my name tab on it, as in my nursery school days. At the meeting for students going to work in Kazakhstan we had been told to sew name tabs on our things. There was a sea of people on the platforms, playing guitars, singing, embracing and crying. Mother was doing her best to keep calm, but when someone nearby asked mournfully, 'Where are they driving those kids?' she burst into tears and could not stop crying. At last we were ordered to get inside, and climbed into our *teplushki*, heated goods vans sometimes used for transporting people. The huge sliding doors were closed, and the train moved off. It was almost dark inside. The only windows were narrow slits at the top, and everyone rushed to try and wave goodbye through them. By standing on a shelf I craned my neck and caught a brief glimpse of Mother in the distance, running, crying and shouting something. Natan was walking behind her with his hand raised. I tried to wave back, but slipped off the shelf.

When my eyes got used to the semi-darkness, I could see the three rows of bunks in the van. For some reason I wound up on the very top, where it was stuffy and I had nightmares. On the second day, fed up with the dark, we managed to slide the door open and the light came streaming in. Fields, forests and villages flashed past. One day we passed a densely forested hill with hundreds of fires blazing on the hillside. A terrifying, but splendid sight.

Most of the boys spent the whole day sitting on the edge of the van with their legs hanging out. The train sometimes raced along, sometimes crawled, and sometimes stood for ages in the middle of some blossoming meadows. We would jump down and run around picking bunches of flowers, which were like the ones in the Moscow countryside, but brighter, larger and somehow more primeval. Our frolicking soon came to an end. The guards marched up and ordered the doors to be shut. Apparently there had been an accident in one of the carriages. A passing train had sliced off someone's leg. This accident and all the subsequent ones (of which there were many) was discussed in blank, hollow tones and the names of the victims were never given.

The train was incredibly long. It was carrying students from various departments of the Institute of Foreign Languages and perhaps some other institutes as well. The five bizarre days we spent on it were a singular experience. Time ceased to exist in the semi-darkness. We never knew where we were going, when we would stop or how soon we would set off again. One day we were woken up in the middle of the night, told to take our bowls and spoons and led off to be fed. Stumbling along sleepily, silent and glum, we came to an empty barrack-like canteen, where some noodles and tough meat were slopped into our bowls. The following night we were awakened by shouts: 'The Ural!' And there it was. I don't remember the banks or the river itself. Only the sensation of the mighty torrent of ice-cold water into which I plunged with a mixture of delight and dread: the night, the strange surroundings, the swift current. We all dived in right in our clothes. 'All aboard!' came the shouts from the bank and we scurried back. Then we spent hours rummaging around for dry clothes in the dark, teeth chattering.

I don't remember at what geographical point my friend and

I found ourselves in a wooden peasant house where we were treated to some delicious sour milk and home-made bread. The woman of the house in a flowery apron first led us to a barrel where she scooped out water with a patterned ladle and splashed it over our hands, then offered us an embroidered towel. On the way back to the train we got lost and ended up between two other trains. One of them was full of boys from a vocational school. 'Hey, get those birds!' they shouted. The boys whistled and ran after us. One of them almost grabbed hold of us, while another tried to trip us up. We turned round, but the way back was blocked as well. I pulled my friend down with all my force and we dived under the train. It was a risky thing to do: these work-camp trains were unpredictable and might move off at any moment. Wriggling out on the other side, we rushed off to find our lot. There they were, the familiar faces. How nice and welcoming they all looked. Diving into our van, we collapsed onto the bunks, doubled up with laughter mixed with sobs. Everyone stared at us in amazement, but we could not stop.

On the sixth day we arrived. There were two lorries to meet us. Our luggage, rucksacks, sacks of dried vobla fish, canned meat and jelly briquettes, were loaded onto one of them, and we piled into the other. The road was full of potholes, and we got bumped about so much that we almost went flying. Clinging to the seat and squinting against the strong wind, we yelled the song: 'I cannot say where we shall meet / Or whether it will be soon / The world goes round and round, my friend, / Just like a blue balloon / Countries and towns are flashing by / But where shall we meet, you and I...'

At last we were there. In the endless steppe stood a vast

tent, big enough for a hundred people. It was divided into two halves: one for the boys and the other, separated by a thin partition, for the girls. I found myself between the partition and one of the girls who snored loudly at night. After I saw her catch a hen and wring its neck this snore began to sound particularly sinister.

Thus I acquired a new address for the next three and a half months: North Kazakhstan, Kokchetav Region, Krasnoarmeisky District, P. O. Box Bolshoi Izyum, Taincha, Station No. 11, elevator. What that all meant was the boundless steppe, feather grass, wormwood and the constantly changing colours of the huge sky that you could observe non-stop. Which is what I did, as I slept very little and walked around for hours on end at night. Not alone either, but with a boy in my year. We got talking on the train and made friends at Station No. 11. 'Do me a favour, come for a walk,' I said to him on one of the first evenings.

There was no work for us to do yet. It was depressing in the tent. I couldn't read and felt lonely and restless. We wandered in the steppe. The feather grass swayed in the wind, and there was a smell of wormwood I picked and sniffed, rubbing it between my palms. We talked endlessly. It turned out that we knew the same people in Moscow, and that we liked the same music, the same books. In short, we were fated to meet.

'Look, look, look at the stars above, / Look, look at my sweetest love, / Oh, dear, give me a night in June, I mean it...' As I sang this old English song, he looked at me, his blue eyes shining, and laughed. 'Sing it again. The way you say "look, look, look" sounds so sweet.' Only work kept us apart. When there was no grain to load into the elevator, they sent us to the collective farm to weed carrots. The lorry took us there early in the morning and brought us back in the evening. Lunch consisted of a plate of milk soup with noodles and a mug of milk. By the end of the week we were ravenous.

Hearing that in Taincha, about 25 kilometres away, there was a canteen where you could get delicious thick cream my friend and I put rubber boots on our bare feet (so they wouldn't get too hot) and set off. We walked for six hours till our feet were raw and bleeding, then in the end took off our boots and finished the walk barefoot. The canteen was empty. We each took a glass of cream and chose a cosy spot at the window with a tulle curtain. Our feet hurt dreadfully and our stomachs were empty. We dipped our aluminium spoons slowly into the rich white cream, savouring each mouthful. Another spoonful, then another and another. Then we had a break. After the break we tried to continue, but soon stopped again. It was much too rich. We looked down at the cream, which had lost all attraction for us, and did not know what to do with it. It would be a pity to leave it there, but we couldn't take it with us. We had nothing to put it in. Trying to avoid the eyes of the woman at the serving hatch, we hobbled out of the canteen.

How on earth were we to get back. We hadn't the strength to cover the twenty-five kilometres barefoot and without our former incentive. We stepped into the roadway and tried to hitch a lift. A lorry stopped. At the wheel sat a smiling young lad. We climbed up next to him and heaved a sigh of relief: thank goodness, he'd take us all the way. No such luck! The driver stank of alcohol, and the lorry was swerving all over the place. When we asked him to stop, he just pressed on the accelerator.

Only when my friend tried to open the door, did he brake suddenly. 'Silly twits,' he shouted after us. 'Nut cases!' At least we had been given a lift part of the way. It was dark before we got back.

Soon the grain arrived and work began in earnest. There were three shifts. At the appointed time we went to the office and were dispatched to one of the grain dryers where the lorries drove up with the grain. At the busiest period there was an endless stream of lorries: we hardly had time to unload one before the next arrived, with a third behind it and so on. And the following day it started all over again: you woke up, pulled on your boots with bits of grain stuck all over the inside, put on your padded jacket, grabbed a pair of mittens and off to the elevator. There was your dryer and your endless row of lorries. You picked up your shovel, climbed over the side of the lorry and shovelled away until you had emptied the lorry of all the grain, which dropped down onto a conveyor belt with sharp blades and was carried off to the elevator. Meanwhile the drivers had a nap. At the height of the harvest season they had to work round the clock and took advantage of any opportunity to get some sleep. We talked about the lorries as if they were living creatures: this one was our favourite, that one was not bad, but that one was horrid. The not bad one was an ordinary lorry, the favourite a tip-up that unloaded itself without our help. And the horrid one was a tip-up lorry with a defect, a body that would not tip up high enough to unload itself but went too high for you to keep your balance in it. Particularly as the floor of the tip-up was slippery. You stood in it, shovelling away, but gradually sliding down, so that any minute you might fall onto the conveyor belt and under the sharp blades. There was a rumour that this had actually happened to one of the students in Taincha. As always nobody told us anything. One day I was working in a pair with a thin, lanky boy who had to cling to me to keep from sliding down in our faulty tip-up lorry: 'Oh, help, I'm falling, oh, Lara, hold me!' That night he kept shouting in his sleep. He must have been dreaming about the lorry.

At the end of the working day my arms, legs and back were numb. But after a short rest I managed to get my strength back from somewhere to go for walks or even to the cinema, which meant slogging several kilometres across the steppe to the next village. And what a cinema it was too! The posters had mistakes in almost every word. 'Funfare of Love' and 'Golden Sinfoni'. There was dancing before the film. With dead-pan faces the local lads, dressed in long jackets and caps, holding their partners close and working hard with their jutting elbows, moved briskly over the crowded floor covered with the husks of sunflower seeds. Everyone chewed seeds, dancers and bystanders alike, also during the film. The more exciting the plot, the more rapid the jaw movement.

The films were like a dream, a wonderful mirage. I have a vague memory of a mountain resort, a posh hotel, a happy love affair, and a beautiful young lady on figure skates performing the most incredible pirouettes on the blue ice. And the music! The heavenly music to go with this heavenly life. Kicking off our boots and opening our jackets, my boyfriend and I sat in the crowded village cinema, gazing entranced at the screen. Yes, this was just the right sort of thing to show at Station No. 11 lost in the steppe. It was about us. The fact that the film was foreign did not matter. It was about us, all the same, about the life that would begin as soon as we were back in Moscow. The Moscow streets, the blue trolley-buses, Sokolniki Park, the gas heater in our communal apartment, the hot shower, Granny's fried potatoes — all this was the same sort of remote dream, a golden symphony, as the magic land of mountain resorts, smart hotels and pirouettes on the ice.

By September, we were living in local people's homes. Eight of us were in the house of the elevator manager. We slept on mattresses on the floor with our clothes on. Everyone had different shifts, morning, afternoon or night. When our shift began at two o'clock in the morning, the previous shift banged on our window to wake us up. The first thing I did after I woke up was to powder my nose in the dark, a substitute for washing. Working on the night shift, I never got enough sleep, and by the end of the second week I began to hear things. In the grinding and scraping of the conveyor belt I heard Mother's voice 'My darling girl,' or Granny calling 'Lara, dear!' Sometimes we managed to have a nap in the office by a white stove big enough for several people to lean against. Once I was woken up by someone shaking my shoulders. Opening my eyes sleepily, I suddenly realised that my back was very hot and there was a smell of burning. 'You're on fire', someone shouted. I tried to take off my jacket, but my fingers would not obey me. The others helped me, and I saw that in one place it was actually burnt. I looked like an old hand in my scorched jacket.

But the hardest time of all was when the trains arrived and we had to load and unload the grain. We crawled into a dark, stifling truck and shovelled the grain scoop by scoop onto a conveyor belt. And so on all day. One of the boys got so tired that he fell asleep on a pile of grain. He was on loading duty. The grain had to be evenly spread all over the truck. While he was asleep it piled up relentlessly. When the other boy came back from lunch he had to dig out his friend who was almost unconscious and coughing blood.

Strangely enough, these accidents did not disturb the ordinary course of our life in the steppe, either because the people in charge always tried to cover them up, or simply because of our childish thoughtlessness.

It was probably because of this thoughtlessness that certain things barely reached my awareness. For example, it never occurred to me to wonder why there were so many Chechens living in the Kazakh steppes. Why the young Chechens threatened not to let a single Muscovite get out of there alive and why they used to raid our camp, careering round it wildly on bikes, waving whips, or throwing stones with a razor-blade tied to them into the tent. (*On Stalin's decree, Chechens were deported from the Caucasus after the war because of their collaboration with the German invaders.*)

Several times I worked with a pretty, young woman whose surname was also Miller. I enquired in surprise where she had got her name from, she told me she was a German from the Volga. This satisfied my curiosity, and I never thought to ask why and when Germans had landed up in Kazakhstan. (*Germans, who settled in Russia in the 18th century were deported during the war as the German army advanced on the Volga.*)

No, at that time I was interested in quite different things: by observing the night sky at length I had learned to tell the time to within a few minutes. On one occasion, when we were still living in the tent, my boyfriend and I were on night duty (set up because of the Chechen raids). We warmed a kettle on a small iron stove which we had set up by the tent outside, made some strong tea and drank it slowly, watching the sun first set and then rise again. 'You know what, I think I love you,' my boyfriend said to me. 'I don't just think, I know I love you.' He put his lips timidly to mine. 'Virgin lands are a school of life,' I laughed.

The summer came to an end and, oh, how we longed to go home. We were counting the days, expecting to leave very soon, when suddenly they told us we were staying until mid-November. Despairing letters flew to Moscow. Happening to glance at the one my neighbour was writing, I saw the tear-stained *cri de coeur*: 'MUM! DISASTER! WE'RE HERE TILL NOVEMBER!'

Not wishing to upset my family, I wrote a fairly calm letter asking them to send some food and, most important, my blue dress. Not long afterwards I had a message that a parcel had arrived in Tainchi. A boy called Zhenya, who functioned as our postman, went to collect it. When I came back from my evening shift, I saw a box in the middle of the room, inside it was fruit that Mother had sent from Kislovodsk, a resort town in the Caucasus where she was spending her vacation. We arranged the fruit in piles: a pile of apples, a pile of pears and a pile of plums. Now it had to be divided into nine shares. That night I had a painful dream of cutting an apple into nine pieces. A few days later a parcel arrived with my blue dress. How thrilling it was to take off my dreary work clothes and plunge into the cool blue silk! I did up the fasteners and set off for the canteen crammed with hungry students queuing for hot buns. My boyfriend was standing right by the serving hatch, and his shining eyes told me that I was not freezing in my light blue dress in vain. 'Fantastic!' he exclaimed and his buns rolled onto the dirty floor.

We were hungry all the time. Particularly as we always got the same food: porridge and noodles. The dried fish, jelly briquettes and tinned meat we had brought with us had all been consumed long ago. In spite of the hard physical labour I had put on three kilos. 'I can see your fat cheeks from behind,' my boyfriend joked. I only wore my blue dress once, I think. There was no occasion to wear it. And the weather was getting colder.

Around the beginning of September our Komsomol leader, a post-grad from the German Department, called a meeting in the Young Communist Room. 'I know many of you are upset by the delay. What are you unhappy about?' he asked. 'We want to go home', people shouted back. 'That's not a proper answer. Be more specific.' 'It's cold wearing rubber boots.' 'So you just need some warm footwear,' the leader said, jotting it down on his pad. 'What else?' A dissonant chorus of voices answered back. 'Can't hear. One at a time.' 'The lorries that deliver the planks dump them down any old how,' someone shouted. 'One boy almost had his head knocked off the other day.' 'Right, we'll make a note of that: lorries knock down comrades,' the post-grad summarised. 'We're sick of porridge,' someone said. 'Okay, so we'll get you dried fish.' That really undid us. If they were going to buy dried fish, we would be here for ages. Maybe forever.

Then I got a message to go to the post office for a long-distance call from Moscow. At the appointed time my boyfriend and I arrived at the post office, a big log cabin manned by a girl telegraph operator. We waited for ages and had almost given up when suddenly... Moscow. Mother's voice. Questions, tears. 'How are you? What's happening?' What can you say in five minutes? 'You tell me how you are in Moscow. Natan? What about Natan? He's there beside you? No, don't give him the phone. Just say hello to him.' Heavens, I'd completely forgotten about Natan. How could I possibly talk to him from here, from this new life, with my impetuous blonde, blue-eyed boyfriend sitting next to me. 'You look like Van Cliburn,' I told him one day. He looked pleased, and I realised I had hit the nail on the head. Later, back in Moscow, taking part in concerts at the Institute, my boyfriend would rush onto the stage, like Van Cliburn, and perform the same *Reves d'amour* as he did. Van Cliburn was his idol.

In June that year the down from the poplar trees swept through the Moscow streets. The First Tchaikovsky Competition at the Conservatory, the inspired playing of a lanky young American — it was all so recent, yet seemed so long ago. One day we heard the sound of a violin from the black loudspeaker over the elevator gates. It was David Oistrakh. The opening of the season at the Conservatory. We stood, transfixed, under the leaky roof of an abandoned barn with the cold autumn rain pouring down. He put his arms round my shoulders and sang quietly in time with the violin in my ear. Did they really exist, the Conservatory, the metro, telephone calls, quiet evening reading by a table lamp, a hot shower? A hot shower was our greatest dream.

Once a week we went to a tiny, almost toy bathhouse, which could only take eight people. The rest had to wait, some in the cramped dressing room, others on the steps or outside in the fresh air. Some just lazed around. Others did something useful, like practising simultaneous interpreting, for example. The fifth-years would occasionally have contests for the quickest, most accurate oral translation. We, second-year whippersnappers, observed these tournaments admiringly. Watching one of them read a difficult Russian text while another said the same thing in English only a few words behind, I swore to myself that as soon as I got to Moscow I would really get down to it: go to the language laboratory, put on the earphones, surround myself with dictionaries and start gabbling like them. 'The road to hell is paved with good intentions...'

I secretly loved bath-day because of the sponge. My boyfriend and I shared the same sponge, and the moment of handing it over was silent confirmation that he and I were one. But except for that the bathhouse was sheer torment for me. Knowing that the heat would make me feel dizzy, I tried to stay near the door so as to slip into the dressing room when I started to blackout. So I kept going to and fro, and washing took me a long time. There was no time left to wash my long thick hair. Once I went down to the river to wash it. The river was shallow, narrow and very clear. I knelt down and put my hair in the water, but when I soaped it, I found it was full of duck feathers. Looking up, I saw some ducks flying past and the water covered with their feathers. At home I started removing the feathers one at a time. Then I lost my patience and pulled the feathers out with my hair. My thick plaits got thinner and thinner. Granny heaved a great sigh when I got back to Moscow. My long, thick hair had been her pride and joy. They said that even in wartime, when there was plenty else to keep her busy, Granny managed to keep my hair nice by washing, combing out and plaiting it. And now this sorry sight. But, at the age of eighteen, having lost some of my hair and acquired chronic arthritis, I felt like a real labour veteran. This sense of being hard-bitten was fuelled by the virgin lands song, composed by a student in our year to the tune of an old tango.

'When we return I know not / Most likely here we'll all rot, / No laxatives, no thalazole. / They'll bury us here, body and soul. / Under a cross and the vast, empty sky / Many of us already lie. / And the party org. says quietly / As he leaves the village cemetery: / 'Marching to Communism's not as easy / As it first appears to be, see.'

We sang this song on our last day in the virgin lands as we bumped our way in the lorry to the station where a real passenger train awaited us this time. We rushed up and down, and when I eventually chose a seat I realised I had lost my rucksack. Looking out of the window, I saw it slumped forlornly on the platform. I should have gone out and fetched it, but I hadn't the nerve to leave the carriage. What if the train suddenly set off and I was left behind. My boyfriend rushed out of the train onto the platform, grabbed the rucksack and barely had time to jump back on the train before it moved off.

WE'RE GOING HOME. It was hard to believe. 'Hurray!' we shouted and hugged each other. Our dreams began to come true almost at once: they gave us clean sheets. I made up my bed, climbed onto the bunk and gazed out of the window. A wonderful life was beginning. What's more I had some money that I'd earned myself. I wanted to take it back intact to show off at home, so I didn't spend a ruble all three days on the train. My boyfriend and I spent most of the time standing on the platform at the end of the carriage, dreaming of our radiant future.

Moscow appeared all of a sudden. Crowds of people to meet us on the platform. Flowers, shouts, tapping on the window, outstretched arms. I glimpsed Mother's face. With the rucksack on my back, I eventually climbed out of the carriage right into her arms. 'My sweet girl,' Mother laughed and cried. 'Pinch me, so I know I'm not dreaming,' I said. We moved along the platform. I looked back and met the eyes of my boyfriend who was being hugged and squeezed by his relatives. Oh, goodness, we hadn't even exchanged telephone numbers. And the platform loudspeakers were playing: 'I cannot say where we shall meet/ Or whether it will be soon./The world goes round and round, my friend,/Just like a blue balloon./Countries and towns are flashing by/But where shall we meet, you and I...'

With my virgin lands pay Mother and I bought me a brocade dress (black with a red sparkle) and my first pair of high-heeled shoes. The brocade was so stiff I could hardly walk, and I kept keeling over on my high heels. But after the padded jacket and rubber boots this outfit seemed the peak of perfection to me.

I was wearing it THAT evening. 'Someone's come to see you,' Mother said, giving me an expressive look. Struggling with the brocade and tottering from side to side on my high heels, I went into the corridor and saw HIM. 'Goodness me, is it really you, Sir?' I addressed my boyfriend with mock gentility. 'How did you find me?' Seeing the neighbours peeping into the corridor, I pulled him into our room in a hurry. But here too we came under the cross fire of my family's curiosity. After sitting at the table and drinking tea for the sake of propriety, we escaped thankfully into the street and set off we knew not where. In those days you could still wander around Moscow as you liked and talk without having to shout. He told me how he had tried to find me and eventually got my address from an information bureau. It grew dark and the leaves fluttered down as we drifted round the neighbouring streets, returned to my entranceway, went inside and warmed ourselves on the radiators, then went out again and finally said goodbye outside my door, arranging to meet the next day.

The Golden Symphony of Moscow life, about which we had dreamed in the steppes, had begun. The next day we went to a piano concert. There was a crowd by the Conservatory. They said the maestro was ill and the concert had been cancelled. A pity, but never mind. We had the whole evening, a whole life, ahead of us.

Autumn leaves on the avenues in the Arkhangelskoye park. He breathed on my hands to warm them. 'Oh, I nearly forgot. I've got socks for you.' He pulled out of his pocket the warm socks Mother tried to give me when we were leaving. They were very welcome now. So was the thermos with hot tea that we poured into mugs, sitting on a fallen tree in a secluded corner of the park. 'Remember how we made tea on night duty by the tent?' I was remembering that too: the scalding tea, the endless sky with dense clusters of glittering stars that slowly faded, then vanished completely, giving way to the rising colours before dawn.

In my three and a half months in the Kazakh steppes I grew

so used to the space and open air that Moscow seemed stifling when I first got back. I longed for the vast sky, the smell of the steppe, the tall grass. I took back a sprig of dry wormwood and hid it in my pillowcase to take out at night and sniff, homesick for the steppe and the sky, the silent witnesses of our romantic walks.

The post-steppe holidays were drawing to an end. Soon classes would begin. And that meant long journeys in a packed metro, then by tram through Sokolniki past little wooden houses, front gardens and dove-cots, along the endless park fence, past the stop with the sweet name of 'May Clearing' to our more prosaic 'Institute of Foreign Languages'.

Yet there was nothing prosaic about life then. Even the smell of burning was associated with a fleeting encounter with my boyfriend in the canteen. And a tedious lecture on linguistics with the chance to catch his glance in my hand mirror and smile. I just had to sit in the row in front on the left. The long queue for the cloakroom was another chance to stand next to him, twirling the cloakroom check on my finger. And then — the long path through Sokolniki Park that twisted and turned, through bushes and trees, into a clearing, then back into a copse until finally we arrived at the park gates. And heaps of fallen leaves, all golden, at our feet.

Going off home did not mean parting. As soon as I opened the door, the phone rang. 'Haven't you eaten yet? Listen, I've just discovered I can sing your name to Schumann's "Dedication".' He put the receiver down on the piano and played, singing my name.

So life went on, a life in which everything was for the best.

Even being ill, because then he came to see me and read me Edgar Allan Poe in English, copying the intonations of the actor on the tape-recorder in our language laboratory. And a few days later he went with me to see a doctor and as we sat in the long queue we held a competition for the best translation of an English poem. I don't remember the author, only the first lines of my own clumsy translation: 'We are together, and though our path be hard, treacherous and unknown...' Hearing my version he tore up his own and declared me the winner.

The Golden Symphony continued, to the constant accompaniment of falling leaves that rustled, danced in the wind, flew to greet us, spun in the air and fell at our feet. 'You're marvellous. You just don't know how marvellous you are. Only don't let your eyes look sad.' But how could I be sad when everything was so perfect. In the evening we went to *Swan Lake* at the Bolshoi. A famous ballerina, my boyfriend's cousin, was dancing. We had entrance passes but no seats. The theatre was packed. We squeezed into one of the top boxes. He knew the ballet by heart and explained nuances of ballet technique to me, the uninitiated.

When it was over we made our way to the metro in a dense crowd. As we went down the steps, chattering, I could sense that my boyfriend had something on his mind. 'I say,' he began, slowing down. 'Would it be alright if I went back? Maya lives near the theatre. I'd like to drop in and see her. All our lot will be there. You don't mind, do you?' He looked at me guiltily. 'If it would upset you, I won't go, really.' 'Of course I don't mind. You must go,' I replied, as lightly as I could. He gave me a happy peck on the cheek and disappeared.

Sunday morning. The phone rings. 'Listen, you must help me quick. It's Maya's birthday, and I don't know what to give her. Think of something, please.' Another call a minute later. 'Have you thought? No, that won't do,' he said, rejecting my banal suggestion. 'Think again.' Another call. 'Listen, I'm in a panic. I've got to leave soon, and I haven't got a present. What can I do?' I said nothing, feeling guilty and useless. Late that evening another call. 'Listen, I thought of a fantastic present. Only don't be upset. I gave her our Mickey Mouse. Please don't be angry. She was so pleased she even decided to take it on tour. Just imagine, it'll go to America.' I could not believe my ears. He had given away OUR Mickey Mouse, the little mouse in the red hat and orange trousers, with a lead weight in its tummy, the amulet I had cherished for three-and-a-half long months in the steppes, taking it with me in the pocket of my padded jacket wherever I went. In the train from Kokchetav to Moscow I had given it to my friend, saying that it would be our amulet now and we would take it in turns. 'Tell me you don't mind, please.' I hung up without a word.

The Golden Symphony began to change its tone and colour somewhat. It was now late autumn. The rain came, battering the faded leaves to the ground. It got colder. We spent less time walking and more going to films and concerts.

That evening we went to a cinema which no longer exists. It was a nice little place in the centre of Moscow that showed newsreels and documentaries. We saw a film about the first Tchaikovsky Competition at the Conservatory. Again the tall, sensitive, romantic Van Cliburn rushed to the piano. His long nervous fingers touched the keyboard, drowning in it, drawing from it sounds heard many times before but still unique. And there was the musical phrase that my name fitted so well.

'Know what, Mother wants to meet you at last,' my friend announced, as we went outside. 'Let's drop in now. It's not far.' I had been waiting for this moment and dreading it. I knew he lived in a posh block of flats, belonging to the Composers' Union. Some old friends of ours had moved in there not long ago. I had been to their pretentious, expensively furnished apartment, as different as chalk and cheese from their tiny earlier one in a rickety two-storey house in the suburbs. When they moved into the new block, these friends of ours changed just as much as their apartments, and seeing them became as difficult as walking over their shiny parquet floor or sitting at the vast table with a starched tablecloth. I was afraid of this apartment block and did not trust it.

'Don't say no,' my friend said urgently. 'Mother will be offended. There's no point in upsetting her right from the start.' 'Some other time,' I said, weakly. He took me home and phoned his mother from my place to say I had a terrible headache. 'Tell her to take a tablet,' a melodious voice commanded down the phone. 'And you come home. There's no point in staying there if she's got a headache.'

The meeting took place a week later. I felt as if I were going to my execution. The familiar side street, the familiar apartment block, the impressive entrance with the pompous attendant, the spacious lift. And here was their apartment. If only the earth would swallow me up. The door was opened by a shortish, well-groomed woman with bright lipstick and a bun of dark hair on the nape of her neck. She was followed by an elderly respectable-looking gentleman in a white shirt, my boyfriend's stepfather. Introductions, smiles and there I was, in the dining room, at just the sort of table I had feared, a vast one with a starched tablecloth. Over tea and cake there was conversation in which I barely took part. He gave me imploring, anxious glances. At last I managed to blurt out something that seemed to just hang in the air. No, I better keep quiet. Let the others talk. My boyfriend's mother was a professional lecturer. Her words flowed freely and easily. As she talked, she would watch herself in the sideboard glass doors or smile at her husband, who was giving her admiring glances. They had not been married long and that was obvious.

'Come with me. I want to show you something,' my boyfriend said, and I followed him happily, aware of the eyes following me. Seating me on the sofa, he got out a pile of photograph albums, letters and folders and dumped them all on my lap.

The long-awaited moment had come. At last he could show me what he had been telling me about for so long. 'Now who's that?' From the many newspaper cuttings an angelic child with blonde ringlets stared out at me. They were shots from the film *Captain at Fifteen* in which he had been an extra. 'Remember the scene when I throw Jack an apple, and he catches it on his knife. Actually he put another apple on his knife and didn't even try to catch mine. I was most surprised when I saw how it was done and I told everyone that the cinema was just tricks.' He undid a pile of letters and my lap was showered with bits of paper covered with childish scrawls, fan mail from grateful and admiring young cinema-goers. And here were the family albums with the same angelic child sitting on his mother's knee, photographs of relatives, famous and not so famous. We sat hunched over the precious archive, while next to us stood the splendid grand piano, the constant witness to and participant in our endless telephone calls.

Into the room came his mother. 'We're off to see some friends,' she drawled loudly. 'What are your plans?' I raised my head and saw that she was taking off her blouse. In nothing but lacy underwear with her hair down, she wandered round the room, trying on earrings and necklaces, powdering her nose and doing her hair. 'Let's go for a walk,' said my friend.

What a relief it was to be outside at last, how easy to breathe again. I regained my powers of speech. We laughed, chattered and fooled around. He kissed me goodbye and walked off in hurried Van Cliburn style.

The next day we met again as usual after classes. Because of the rain we took the tram instead of walking. As I sat down in a free seat and put his case on my lap, I began telling him something amusing about our group meeting, but then stopped short when I saw the vacant, strange expression in his eyes. 'What's the matter?' I asked anxiously. 'Nothing. I slept badly.' In the metro we said goodbye as we changed trains. He told me his mother had said to come home early. I went home alone. I stood in the carriage, looking at the black windows of the train, until I realised I had gone past my station.

That day the phone was silent. My boyfriend did not ring until late in the evening to say that he had been dreadfully busy doing jobs for his mother: getting books from the library and taking an article to be typed. Then he paused. 'What's happened?' I asked in a flat voice. He said nothing, as if gathering courage.

'When I got back yesterday Mother made a scene, said it was time to stop all this and start studying. I told you not to get on the wrong side of her at the very start. Remember that evening when you refused to come to our place?' I said nothing. 'Don't worry, everything will be the same as before,' he faltered.

But everything was not 'the same as before'. It was apparently the same, but different. Like the game where you have to find ten things that are different in two almost identical pictures. Both had the Grand Hall of the Conservatory with two people sitting in their usual seats in the circle on the left. But in the first he is looking at her and in the second at the stage. In the first he is playing with her fingers, in the second tapping the programme. In the first he hangs on her every word, in the second he doesn't even look at her.

The winter holidays came. He invited me to a play in which his aunt was acting. When I took off my coat, he exclaimed: 'For heaven's sake, what are you wearing? What a dreadful colour!' I was wearing a new dress made from a length of orange-coloured cloth that Granny had been saving for me. I was hoping to impress him with it, and impress him I did. During the interval he begged me not to go into the foyer. 'You can't appear in public in that thing. I won't be a minute.' He reappeared when the lights went down. 'Look what I've brought,' he whispered, dropping a handful of sweets in my lap. A reward for doing as he said.

Then summer came. Mother and I went to Kislovodsk in the Caucasus. We had an active holiday, walking in the hills and going to the library and concerts. But all the time I was waiting for one thing only, when I could go to the post office for mail. He sent two letters. In the first he advised us to go to the place where Pechorin (the hero of Lermontov's *Hero of Our Time*) fought his duel and gave detailed instructions how to find it. In the second and last he told me that his stepfather had died suddenly. 'Mother and I will be very close now,' he wrote.

Then it was autumn again. Metro Sokolniki. The number ten tram. The Institute. He sat in his usual place one row above me, and I could see his face in my mirror. After classes we walked through the park. The familiar pond, the familiar paths. He told me what he had been doing. Asked me questions. The conversation was stilted. 'Why didn't you write more?' We sat down on a bench. 'This year was a very hard one for me, you know. I didn't want to tell you, but each day Mother kept finding fault with you.' 'What faults? She doesn't even know me.' 'That's not important. She talked nonsense: about the way you walk, crooked stocking seams, shabby shoes. But it gets you down when you have the same thing day in day out. I'm sorry, but it's all different now.' I threw back my head to stop the tears. I hadn't the strength to get up. Time passed. 'Come on,' he said quietly, stretching out his hand. We wandered slowly to the metro.

At home as I crossed the threshold, I realised that the telephone would be silent now. No matter who rang. And that there would never be anything else. Nevermore, as in Edgar Allan Poe, whom he had read to me.

When Mother came home that evening she asked anxiously: 'What's the matter?' I said nothing. 'Come here. What's happened?' She sat me down on her lap and began to rock me like a little child. 'Now tell me, tell me quickly.' Then I let go and sobbed my heart out. 'What's the matter, love? It's not because of him, is it? Surely it can't be? You're so young. Your whole life's ahead of you. Now stop crying and tell me what's the matter. What was there between you? Tell me. You couldn't go on like that unless there was something. Tell me what there was.' 'Nothing,' I sobbed. 'There was nothing.' Then I slid down from Mother's lap and stuck my head in a pillow.

Black days went by, then black years. But they were black with a bright thread, like my brocade dress I had stopped wearing long ago. The bright thread was his blue suit that would flash past on the stairs, his shining glance I might catch at a lecture, his smile in the corridor. We rarely spoke. He did not even know how to address me now. He was not used to using my full name and dared not call me by the affectionate one.

One day that autumn I left the institute with a friend. It was raining, cold and slushy. We waited at the stop. Eventually a tram appeared. 'What if I were to throw myself under it?' I asked jokingly. 'They'd all say you did it because HE chucked you.' 'Oh, anything but that,' I thought to myself in horror.

'Oh, how sad, sad, sad I am, how I suffer, suffer, suffer.' The song at the beginning of the Golden Symphony turned out to be prophetic. Although prophetic is hardly the right word. After all, that is what usually happens to first love. Ordinary yet once in a lifetime.

Whereas in the first term I still managed to go to gym lessons, in the second I decided to give them a miss. The reason was that our two groups, mine and my ex-boyfriend's, had unexpectedly been combined. Which meant that BEFORE HIS VERY EYES I would have to hop around the gym with a ball between my feet which would keep rolling away, of course; jump over the horse, never quite clearing it; and climb up the bars to strike a 'swallow' pose with one trembling leg. And there was a new teacher. The one before had been a bald young man who couldn't pronounce his r's and used to call out patiently: 'Spwing, Millew, spwing', in the second term his place was taken by a woman of indeterminate age who we called 'Blue Pants' because of her bright blue track suit. She was a no-nonsense lady who followed the army principle: 'If you can't do it, we'll teach you, if you don't want to, we'll make you.' One lesson was enough for me. After that I spent gym lessons skulking in the library or secretly watching my ex-boyfriend doing perfect press-ups or cavorting gracefully on the bars.

This went on until the spring exams. Then suddenly, a bolt from the blue: I would not be allowed to take the exams because I had no gym test mark. I rushed round looking for Blue Pants in the gym, the staff room and the canteen where eventually I spotted her. Having waited tactfully for her to finish a pastry, I then asked a ridiculous question: 'What can I do about the test?' 'I don't know,' she replied, producing compact and lipstick from her blue pants. 'But they won't let me take the exams.' 'It's your own fault,' Blue Pants replied briskly, applying a thick layer of lipstick.

'Go and see the rector,' one of the students advised me. After waiting in the anteroom, I found myself in a vast office, where behind an enormous desk sat the elderly, grey-haired and narrow-eyed lady rector. 'I'm listening,' she said, looking up from her papers and lifting her glasses. 'They won't let me take the exams because I didn't do the gym test.' 'Why not?' 'I didn't go to the lessons.' 'Why not?' I said nothing. 'Were you ill?' I nodded.

'Then bring a medical certificate.' 'But can I take the test now?' 'Don't ask me. Go and see the teacher.' 'I've already seen her.' 'And what did she say?' I shrugged my shoulders and asked timidly: 'Can't you tell her to let me take the test?' 'Why should I? If you missed the lessons, why tell her to let you take the test?' 'But I want to try and pass it.' 'Then you should have tried earlier. Why did you come to me?' 'I was advised to.' 'Well, it was bad advice.'

Realising that the conversation was over, I went down to the gym again to see Blue Pants. 'Can I take the test?' 'What test?' she exclaimed, obviously enjoying my discomfort. 'The marks have all been entered and handed in. I'm about to retire. So you'll have to manage without me.' Back I went, along the corridor up the stairs to the anteroom and into the rector's office. 'Why have you come back?' I recounted the conversation with Blue Pants. 'Well, what do you expect me to do? We never invent marks. If you were ill, bring a certificate. Otherwise you won't be admitted to the exams.'

On the way home I had one thought only: 'What will Mother say? I can't hide it any longer.' As I expected, Mother was furious. 'How could you? How dare you? I worked myself crazy all that year to pay for coaching so you would pass the entrance exams, and because of this nonsense...' She rushed to the telephone and dialled Granny's number. 'Mother, something terrible's happened. This wretched creature might be thrown out of the institute. Don't shout, just be quiet and listen to me. We need a medical certificate saying she's been ill. Something serious, because she missed a lot of lessons. Ask Paulina Vulfovna. Tell her anything you like, but we must have it at once.' Paulina Vulfovna, Granny's district doctor, a kind soul to whom patients went with complaints not only about their health, but about everything under the sun, wrote out a certificate saying that a bout of flu had produced cardiac complications. I don't remember the exact medical term, but it was most impressive.

Overjoyed at receiving this precious document, I sped back to the Institute. The exams were due to start in two days and I hadn't done any studying yet. All I wanted was to hand the certificate and forget about the whole thing. The institute was cold and deserted. I was in luck. There was no one in the anteroom and the rector was in her office. I went in and solemnly produced my certificate. She took the paper and studied it carefully. 'Who gave you this?' she asked, lifting her head and fixing her eyes on me. I went cold, sensing trouble, and decided not to give any names. 'It's written there.' 'The writing's illegible. What's the surname?' 'I don't remember.' 'Don't you even know the name of your own district doctor?' 'It's not my doctor. I stayed with Granny when I was ill.' 'Oh, you did, did you?' drawled the rector, her thin lips creasing into an ironic smile. 'Well, we'll soon find out who the doctor is. So you had flu and it was followed by complications. If that's the case, you must have missed quite a few lessons in other subjects as well. We'll check that now. Milochka,' she called the secretary. 'Get me the class register for group 205 and ask the nurse to come here with Miller's card.' All this was like a bad dream in which a new character now appeared, a lame hunchback in a white coat, fully in keeping with bad dreams. She was famous for diagnosing each student who entered her office: 'Deliberate malingering.' Looking at me, the way a boa constrictor might survey a rabbit, she placed a folder on the rector's desk. The rest I don't remember. All I can recall is the end of the dream and the metallic voice that announced: 'Well, it's quite clear now. You never had any flu, you missed no lessons except gym and you did not complain about your heart. Your certificate is false and will stay here. You can go. We'll let you know when we need to see you.' My legs felt rooted to the ground. 'Anything else?' asked the rector. 'Can I take the exam the day after tomorrow?' I asked, mouthing the words with difficulty. The rector banged her pen on the desk, leaned back in her chair and burst into satanic laughter. 'Exam, she says! You're in possession of a forged document! You should be taken to court!' Then she stopped laughing and added in a matter-of-fact tone: 'The exclusion order will be issued tomorrow. Then we'll have a meeting of the Institute and decide what to do with you. You'll be expelled from the Komsomol, of course, and then we'll see. No more questions? You can go.'

I don't remember how I left the institute and got home or what I told Mother. All I do remember is finding myself in the street again after a while, only not alone, but with Mother. We walked to the metro, took a train to Sokolniki, then a tram and got off at the institute. Mother went into the rector's office without me. I waited in a dark corner of the corridor. Mother was gone for ages. She finally reappeared and set off for the exit, without turning to look at me. I followed her. We walked to the tram stop in silence. Suddenly she swung round and slapped my face. 'You wretch!' she sobbed. 'Because of you I had to grovel, go down on my knees, crawl.' I watched her in silence, then suddenly burst into tears. For the first time since it all began I cried, choking with sobs, and could not stop. A tram drew up.

We sat down on the back seat and Mother whispered, hugging me by the shoulders: 'Calm down, it's alright now. The medical certificate's been torn up. We were lucky. While I was talking, the deputy rector came into the office. She turned out to be a very nice person. When I went down on my knees, she ran over to pick me up, and when she heard that your father had been killed at the front and I had brought you up on my own, she went to the desk and tore the certificate into shreds. "Tell her to come and do the exams," she said. "I take responsibility for everything." '

I did well on the exams, but at each one the rector appeared ghost-like in the examination room, smiling her thin bloodless smile and shaking her finger at me. As if afraid I might forget her.

My Romance with English

In the early stages, my relationship with English was most dramatic: it consisted entirely of non-meetings (if I may be forgiven for using Akhmatova's word in such a frivolous context). The first non-meeting took place in the early fifties in the village of Rastorguyevo, where Granny's kindergarten spent the summer months. That summer I was not staying with the children, but with Granny in her room in the teachers' quarters. The latter included a child carer who knew English. She had with her an adapted version of *Oliver Twist* with the help of which she regularly tormented her own son and later, at Granny's request, me too. Poor Oliver aroused nothing but pity in me. Pity not for him, but for myself. As if school were not enough, I had to sit on a stuffy veranda stupidly repeating English words from Dickens, while the other children were laughing and squealing outside on this lovely summer day.

The second non-meeting was when we got back to Moscow. *Step by Step*, my stepfather solemnly read the title of the large tattered tome from which he himself had once attempted to learn English. Home tuition had begun. 'This is a carpet,' he said, poking at our carpet hanging on the wall. 'This is a table,' he announced, banging his hand on our table. 'Three little pigs,' he explained, pointing at a picture in the book. All the words were pronounced loudly and zestfully, but he took special pleasure in those with an inter-dental 'th', which he replaced with an 's' or a 'z' for simplicity's sake. Mother was delighted: now in addition to school I was getting an extra chunk of English at home. She herself, in spite of some mythical Berlitz courses which she had once attended, could not help me. The English words that she uttered occasionally sounded so strange and made me so confused that she lapsed into guilty silence. The school English that produced all these additional efforts I have totally forgotten.

My first and last memories of it date back to 1953, the year of the 'Doctors' Plot'. The English teacher in our class, Sofia Nahumovna, was a shortish woman with a pleasant face and thick hair streaked with grey. When the anti-Jewish campaign started with denunciatory articles in the press, she was so nervous she could hardly teach. I felt that she was particularly afraid of the cheeky, spiteful girls (of which there were quite a few in our class) and tried to ingratiate herself with them by giving them high marks. At that time she hardly noticed me.

This constituted all my early English. How I came to enter the Foreign Languages Institute I do not know. Actually, the reason is quite clear. I always found English easier than other subjects. The chemistry teacher called me a 'blockhead'. The maths, physics and drawing teachers probably thought the same, but were more restrained. With history, particularly ancient history, everything would have been fine, if it were not for names and dates. And literature... Ah, literature, that was a different kettle of fish. I loved it, but not the school literature, that special mix prepared by the textbook author and my teacher, who rewarded any departure from the strict school syllabus with a merciless bad mark. Composition was the barrier I did not manage to clear at the entrance exams to the Philology Department of Moscow University.

Ah, that hot summer of 1957! The cool metal steps of the university staircase where I sat in a trance, unable to find my name in the list of those admitted to the next exam. Ah, that hot summer of the World Youth Festival, an event that passed me by completely, because after failing the university entrance exams, I made a desperate attempt, at Mother's insistence, to get into the Foreign Languages Institute. The one exam I do not remember was the English exam (another non-meeting). Yet I do remember taking the oral history exam perfectly. I drew ticket 29 ('The triumphal progress of Soviet power' and 'Stepan Razin's Peasant Uprising'), the one I was dreading because I hadn't reviewed it and only managed to go through it just before the exam, waiting for my turn in the stuffy corridor.

Here I was at the Foreign Languages Institute or Inyaz as it's called for short. This, logically speaking, was when my meeting with English should have taken place. Yet life is more powerful than logic or, at least, it's quite a different kettle of fish. Inyaz was many things for me, except the mastery of English.

Inyaz was, first of all, an escape from hated school, a dizzy sense of something new, intelligent teachers who treated you as an adult. Inyaz was heart-to-hearts with girlfriends, happy idling away the time and equally happy swotting together for exams. Inyaz was not so much Chaucer, Shakespeare and Byron, as the jazz songs we sang with abandon, so that our parties attracted Moscow's 'golden' youth. Inyaz was a love that made the institute the happiest and later the unhappiest place in the world.

But what about English? What about our wonderful teachers fanatically in love with English, including assorted Americans or, rather, American Jews whose high-minded ideological beliefs had brought them to Russia in the thirties. Surely their efforts were not in vain? And what about my regular visits to the Foreign Languages Library, where the inimitable Vladimir Pozner gave talks on new English and American literature? Surely all that was not in vain? Probably not. Probably I did absorb some of it in spite of myself. But so much less than I could have. Looking back, I see that in my student years my romance with English kept waning and flaring up again with new strength. In the first year the idea of learning English seemed most attractive. My friend and I vowed to speak English to each other every day. And made a most energetic start. Surrounded by dictionaries, we tried to discuss a new play. Yet our thoughts and emotions were so much richer than our vocabulary that we gradually slipped back into Russian.

Inyaz taught bookish English and also provided a broader linguistic education. We had lecture courses on the history of the English language, linguistics, phonetics, psychology and literature. True, they also subjected us to 'historical and dialectical materialism' and the history of the Communist Party. Much time went to Teaching Methods and practice at school, which I swallowed like bitter medicine. Yet all the same no historical materialism or teaching practice could prevent someone who really wanted to from mastering the language. In spite of the academic nature of the teaching and virtual absence of any contact with the spoken language, you could learn a lot in your five years at the Institute. Even if it was by the unusual method that our teacher Vengerov used as a student. He used to turn up at a teachers' hostel in Petroverigsky Lane, find a native speaker and ask permission to sit quietly in a corner and listen to them talking. In that way he managed to immerse himself in the spoken language.

Sometimes, in one of my bursts of enthusiasm for English, I would sit in the language laboratory, listening to extracts from the classics read by English actors and even learning some of them by heart. Edgar Allan Poe's famous 'Bells' was my favourite. But all of this was like a dream. Too many other things were happening to me in those years: eternal friendship, love to the grave, the collapse of the former and the latter, and also a constant search for the meaning of life. Which does not lie in the study of English, of course. And so it all went on until something happened that made me sit up and take notice. One day I needed my English teacher's signature on a document and suddenly realised I did not know how to ask for it in English. Feeling an almost physical disgust with myself, I decided to begin a new life forthwith.

And begin it I did. Following the example of other students in my year, I began to search out 'native speakers' and make up for the lack of spoken English by talking to them in informal settings. My first catch was the sister of the famous violinist Yehudi Menuhin, a pianist who came with him on a concert tour. This lady's husband had a psychiatric clinic either in the States or in England, and she asked me to accompany her to a Moscow psychiatric hospital where she had been promised a meeting with the head doctor. Entering the hospital we were immediately stopped by some rude shouts coming from a figure in a white coat, yelling at us that we had come in through the wrong door. My companion was most upset. 'What does he want? What's the matter?' At the sound of English speech, the man stopped in his tracks, gaping. Taking advantage of the pause, I explained to him who we were and why we had come. After that everything was like a corny film: bowing and smiling, the man took us to the head doctor's office. The transformation was so sudden it was embarrassing. 'How nasty,' the lady kept repeating. 'It's all because I'm a foreigner. How nasty.'

My next catch was an American couple who had come for the International Oncologic Congress, a surgeon by the name of Norman and his wife Mildred. I met them when I was registering the congress participants at the Ukrainé Hotel. Petite little Mildred talked only about her four children, while lanky Norman, swathed in photo and film cameras, wanted to know everything about Russia. Noticing a woman carrying a huge bundle on her back, he demanded: 'Larissa, go up and ask what's in her sack.' He was most disappointed when I said that would be rude. At the sight of a drunk asleep on the pavement, he got out his camera and tried to photograph him, thereby arousing the indignation of patriotic passers-by. To my intense embarrassment he put his foot on the bus seat to do up his shoe lace, and to my great delight whistled a perfect rendering of Grieg's piano concerto and other classics. When we said goodbye they confessed that, not understanding why anyone would work for nothing, they had been afraid at first that I was KGB, but had stopped worrying when they got to know me better.

The most significant event in my 'English' life was working at the British Trade Fair in Sokolniki in 1961. This was my first officially sanctioned activity, for which I even got paid at the end of the two weeks. Arriving at the 'Electronics' stand I found myself in the company of some very nice gentlemen. I remember three of them: tall, skinny Geoff, elegant Mr Willoughby and a stocky elderly gentleman of Semitic appearance. Sentimental Geoff was impressed by everything, the birch trees in the park, the pigeons by the university, and my long plaits. Little Mr Willoughby in his expensive three-piece suit with a pipe in his mouth, was constantly expressing the desire to travel round the USSR and kept repeating the names of towns which sounded as magic words: 'Omsk, Tomsk, Minsk'. This passion led him one day to the Belorussian Station, where he succumbed to his wanderlust, got on a suburban train and travelled for several stations. He then related his brave adventure with the pride of a child who had run away from home. The elderly gentleman of

Semitic appearance kept trying to get me on my own to ask me how Jews lived in the USSR. One day he managed to trap me in a corner and block all means of retreat: 'They say there's a lot of anti-Semitism in your country. And that it's hard for Jews to get a higher education. Is that true?' 'Well, I'm a college student as you can see,' I said, trying to break out of the trap. This elicited the following derisive comment from Mr Willoughby: 'Russian girls have all the answers.'

One day when I was handing out brochures to visitors at the exhibition, I noticed a man watching me. Thinking he wanted a brochure, I went up to him and heard him whisper: 'Someone will be waiting for you at six fifteen on the bench by the pavilion.' Without quite understanding what was going on, I realised that I had to do as he said and turned up at the appointed place and time.

To my amazement the person sitting on the bench was a recent Inyaz graduate, Tolya Agapov. I felt a great sense of relief: good-hearted, smiling Tolya with his broad face and dimpled cheeks could not possibly represent a threat. And his manner towards me did indeed seem friendly and open. It turned out that Tolya had been sent to work at the KGB after he graduated and was now acting in an official capacity sitting on the bench with me. He asked me about 'my' Englishmen, what they said and where they went. When I forgot to mention a walk with Geoff in Lenin Hills, he reminded me about it. 'If you know everything why ask me?' I said in surprise. 'To make you feel responsible,' he explained without a smile. 'And in general be careful. It's a tricky business... you don't want to get in a mess,' he added confidentially, lowering his voice. A few years later I heard that he had started drinking heavily and later committed suicide. Suicide was the last thing you would have expected from him. Obviously the work had not suited him.

On the last day of the exhibition I was called to a special room and told to write a report, that is, to put down in writing everything I had told Tolya. 'Ah, the great Russian language,' the language of our KGB, so zealously protecting me from excessive contacts with English. 'Ah, the great Russian language,' into which I had to translate those simple English dialogues. This experience cooled my ardour considerably and diminished my desire to meet 'native speakers'. Nevertheless working at the exhibition was my first real MEETING with English. I saw that it could be used to make jokes, to be sad or sentimental, to order food in the cafe, to rhapsodise about the ballet, or to talk about your family and your cat. All this not in the tedious cliches from our textbooks. And not in the old-fashioned English of Dickens and Galsworthy, that we studied in class.

Eight years later, in spite of everything, I agreed to work in Sokolniki again. I was told that they needed an interpreter urgently for an international exhibition that had already opened. The next day I was back in the familiar park and even the same pavilion. This time my boss turned out to be a tall, broad-shouldered young German who lived in the States and represented an American company. He greeted me curtly, told me briefly about the exhibits and sat down to read his paper. Each morning began with my boss running his finger distastefully over the desk and exhibits and then holding it up for me to see. Realising that I was not prepared to draw the expected conclusions, he grumbled: 'Your duties include dusting, sweeping and making coffee.' If he had asked me politely I might have agreed. 'I was sent here as an interpreter,' I replied. 'Who by? The KGB?' he shouted. 'They took one away — she was not a good informer. And now they've sent you. That's true, isn't it?' 'I didn't know I was taking someone's place,' I began, then I saw it was hopeless to try and justify myself. He was getting more and more agitated. 'I suppose these walls are bugged, eh? They told us everything before we came here. One, two, three, four, five,' he shouted unexpectedly, addressing the ceilings and walls. 'I don't want to end up in Siberia, see? I'm not afraid of you.' Then turning to me again: 'Why did you allow your government to send troops to Czechoslovakia?' 'No one asked me,' I replied. 'Well, they should have,' he countered. 'Did they ask you when they massacred the Jews in Germany?' He stopped short, paused, then said sombrely: 'The nation went mad.' It was obvious that my question had upset him. He began to explain that although he had not been alive then, he too felt a burden of guilt. From then onwards my German became slightly more pleasant and talkative with me and even permitted himself the occasional smile. Nevertheless each morning he would greet me with the same question: 'Writing reports, eh?' With regard to these 'reports' nobody told me to write them until the very last day. 'Why haven't you submitted a single report?' I was asked after being summoned to the same room as in 1961. So I had to write my one and only report after all, it consisted of some brief information about the company and its exhibits.

While I was writing it an interpreter from a neighbouring stand ran into the room holding a sheet of paper. Her cheeks were burning and she was in tears. From her somewhat incoherent account I gathered that a letter with a request for political asylum had been left on her stand. This caused a great stir with people running in and out and making phone calls. I fled. 'No more exhibitions,' I decided.

A few years later I made the acquaintance of two very nice post-graduate students from England. One was called Cynthia and the other Wendy. Cynthia was a bit lazy about speaking Russian and always glad to switch into English, but hard-working Wendy took every opportunity to practise her Russian. I became friendly with both of them, but Cynthia left earlier, and Wendy stayed on a few more months. My friendship with her was a great blessing to me. For the first time I was able to speak not simply with a native speaker, but with someone who shared my interests. At last I had a chance to speak English (we agreed to speak Russian part of the time and then English) about what really mattered to me — literature, the theatre, education, traditions. Unfortunately this experiment also ended in disaster. My husband was suddenly summoned to the dreaded 'First Department' at work where a very large young man, Edik from the Lubyanka, explained that Wendy was more than just a post-graduate student and 'asked' most insistently that we should continue our contacts with her and report everything.

All we could do after that was inform our friend that she was on the blacklist. But how? There were eyes and ears everywhere. At last I had the bright idea of inviting her to a place where she had probably never been before and which was unlikely to be bugged — the Central Baths. 'A brilliant idea,' I congratulated myself as we went inside. But in the dressing room a young blonde woman settled down next to us, who seemed to be listening to every word we said (we were speaking Russian so as not to attract attention). This worried me and I decided to postpone my important announcement until the steam room. But we didn't manage to talk there either. Overwhelmed by the heat, the steam and the sight of lobster red bodies being flagellated with birch twigs, my friend turned pale and began to wilt. I caught hold of her and led her out. After sitting the poor girl on a bench and giving her a chance to recover, I overwhelmed her yet again and much more strongly than before. As she listened to my account, she kept saying: 'Oh no, oh no.' Then in agitated, rapid English she began questioning me, thanking me and lamenting: 'So they'll never let me back again, never let me back.' We said a tearful farewell, convinced that we were parting forever.

Only twenty-two years later did we happen to meet again. I got a long, detailed letter from Wendy saying that she was teaching Russian at Nottingham University, writing articles and books on Russian literature, including one on Anna Akhmatova, that she remembered our talks, my three-year-old son and my Granny's curd dumplings.

My romance with English was pretty hard going. Not only because of the occasional 'uninvited third party', but also for purely private reasons: my long search for a meaning in life had led me to begin writing poetry and everything connected with English was an obstacle to this. Particularly the school where I was sent to work after graduation. It threatened to devour me body and soul: the preparation for lessons, the children who had to be indulged, taught and kept in hand, the staff meetings, the marking. And so on each day.

One afternoon when I was leaving the school a timid woman

came up to me. 'Excuse me,' she said shyly, 'but my son Filip has been getting up at crack of dawn for a week to revise the poem you set for homework. Please ask him to recite it.' Goodness me, how could I have forgotten him? I don't remember how I got through that night. As soon as I entered the classroom, I asked the little lop-eared second-former to come out in front of the class. Nervously swallowing his words and speaking too quickly, he rattled off the poem and got top marks. As I watched him carry his class diary with the precious 'five' and put it carefully on his desk and saw his shining face and bright red ears I thought to myself: 'What would have happened if his mother hadn't reminded me? I must leave here quickly before I do any real harm.' The head teacher secured my release before my obligatory three years were up. In parting she said to me: 'Well, off you go, we don't need travellers in transit. But remember: if you can't work in a school, you won't be able to write poetry.'

All my subsequent teaching took place in the evening: English at night school, an extra-mural course at a polytechnic institute, and, finally, evening classes in the history department of Moscow University. I had gone the full circle and here I was again in the old university building on Mokhovaya Street. This time not as a would-be student who had failed the entrance exams, but as a teacher. In front of me stood a handsome dark-haired and dark-eyed young man, my student, who said firmly, but with a slight stutter: 'I can't go home without passing the test. Mother couldn't stand it. She's got a weak heart.' 'But I can't give you a pass mark. You don't know anything,' I replied just as firmly. 'But I won't go away, I just can't.' 'Alright then,' I gave in. 'I'll put down a pass mark. But it's for your mother, not for you. I'll give you one when you've learnt enough. The mark is only valid when it's transferred to the official list. So I advise you to get a move on.' The student had not expected events to take this turn and was at a loss for words. I was pleased with myself for having found a solution without compromising my noble vocation or being too heavy-handed.

What does teaching a foreign language to technical students mean? It means 'topics' and 'thousands'. Topics such as 'My Town', 'My Family' and 'My Working Day', and 'thousands' being the one thousand characters that constitute the length of the specialist text each student has to read and translate. Excruciatingly boring. I tried to liven things up by teaching spoken English and bought some amusing little books at the 'Druzhba' bookshop in Gorky Street for this purpose. It was fun seeing the attitude of my students gradually change. When I first started teaching them, they took one contemptuous look at me (I looked younger than most of them) and decided to give me the works, by skipping lessons, arriving late and chatting loudly during classes. But as soon as they realised I meant business and was giving them the chance to learn something, they were transformed. Apparently there is a potential hardworker and enthusiast inside every idler.

Eventually the small lecture hall was packed to overflowing. Even students from other groups came. How was I to cope with these numbers? I couldn't turn them away. The main thing was to keep up the pace: question, answer, another question, short text reading, comprehension check, improvised conversation, reading in parts, another question. After one of these sessions a plumpish student with a flushed face came up to me and said happily: 'Phew, I'm sweating like a pig. It even makes you lose weight.'

I stopped teaching officially in 1972 when my second son was born, and had to give private lessons instead.

However, my real romance with English was just beginning. And this time it began as it was supposed to, right at the beginning, with nursery rhymes and riddles, *Mother Goose* and *Brer Rabbit*, absurd and sentimental songs, tongue-twisters and fables, the pig that could fly and the cow that jumped over the moon, the old woman who lived in a shoe and the crooked man who bought a crooked cat with a crooked sixpence: with delightful pictures showing a baker baking pies and doughnuts and Jack putting in his thumb and pulling out a plum. Here it was, a child's English, as natural and essential as milk teeth.

This was when at last I met 'good old England', where Wee Willie Winkie runs through the town in his nightgown to make sure that all the boys and girls are in their beds. There it was, the 'good old England', I should have discovered years ago as a child, when instead I was made to read about a little revolutionary girl called Tanya, sing songs about Lenin and later learn the political vocabulary for holding a conversation on 'The USSR, a bulwark for peace on earth.'

I had at last arrived at the English language with which young Vladimir Nabokov began. It was not so much my meeting as my children's. For their sake I got together children's groups which I taught for almost ten years. Progressing from nursery rhymes to Byron's poetry, from *Brer Rabbit* to Rudyard Kipling, from a play about the *Little Red Hen* to Oscar Wilde's *The Importance of Being Earnest*. We traversed the long path from *Old Macdonald* to *My Fair Lady* and *Jesus Christ Superstar*.

We would have gone further, if not for the ill-fated 1983. That November I started rehearsing Bernard Shaw's *Augustus Does His Bit* for the Christmas concert. I remember dying of laughter as I read the play and imagined my children laughing. But it turned out to be no laughing matter at all.

On 17 November our flat was searched and as well as confiscating material connected with my husband's civil rights activities they took away all my English tapes and a great deal more for good measure. The search went on until eight in the evening, and at seven there was a ring at the door from pupils whom I had not been able to warn in advance. They were interrogated as well, of course, their names and addresses written down. The lesson took place, but it was the last one. The children's parents decided not to take any risks, which was only natural in those days.

My Land and Home

At the age of six a little boy next door declared his love for me and offered to catch butterflies together. Seeing this his mother took him away. He never approached me again, but one day as he was running past, he pulled my braid and squeaked: 'I won't play with Jews.'

In 1953, the year of the 'Jewish Doctors' Plot', I was in the seventh year at school. Of the three rows of desks in the classroom

I occupied one whole row by myself. The other girls used to cram themselves three to a desk in the other two rows. As the only Jewish girl in the class I was ostracised as punishment for the Jewish Doctors. During the breaks they would surround me and push me about like a ball.

A year later, when co-education had been reintroduced, I was on my way to the toilet with a blackboard cloth in my hand. I was on duty that day. A crowd of boys stampeded down the corridor towards me. As they came alongside, one of them shouted: 'Bloody kike!' in my face and punched me on the head. The world spun, I staggered and leant against the wall, to stop myself falling. When I told Mother about the incident, she asked my stepfather to complain to the headmistress. I was summoned to the head's office, where she and her deputy, the physics teacher Kisselmann, also a Jew, were waiting for me. 'Well, tell us exactly what happened,' the headmistress enunciated solemnly. I told them. 'Are you sure that's what he said?' the headmistress inquired coldly. Kisselmann, who was pitifully flustered, intervened at this point: 'Perhaps you misheard?' The headmistress waited, tapping a pencil on the desk. 'Those were his exact words,' I persisted. 'But you said you nearly fainted,' Kisselmann was almost pleading. 'You must have imagined it.' My eyes filled with tears, and I ran out of the office, cursing myself for bothering to report it. What was the use?

The 1960s. Tram No. 10 from Sokolniki to the Institute of Foreign Languages was always bursting with students. In front of the Institute the noisy crowd would rush off the tram and race to the entrance, trying to get into the auditorium before the lecturer. The middle-aged door-keeper was supposed to check our passes. But she never attempted to do it in the hustle and bustle of the morning rush. In any case she knew all our faces. But whenever I passed by, she invariably grabbed my sleeve and demanded to see my pass. I would start rummaging through my bag, a queue would form, somebody would urge her, 'Let her through, you've seen her a hundred times!' But she would just insist grimly, 'Your pass!' This scene was re-enacted every time this woman was on duty. But one day something in me snapped, I wrenched myself free and marched on. 'Jewish shit,' she hissed after me.

I had grown up hearing such insults, but this time, blind with fury, I turned round and walked back towards her. I might have struck the old bitch if my best friend hadn't come between us, gripped my shoulders and repeated several times: 'Take it easy now... take it easy...' A few days later a notice was put up: I'd been deprived of my monthly stipend for 'hooliganism'.

My city. My street. My house.

House-painters were working in our entranceway. I went downstairs to collect the post from our mailbox. One of the young painters, sitting on a window sill for a smoke, said with an insolent grin: 'Pretty eyes. Pity they're Jewish.' Suddenly I choked with rage. 'You ought to be ashamed of yourself! My father volunteered for the front and was killed in action before you were even born!' My voice broke. The young man stared at me and shifted uncomfortably in his seat. My outburst had taken him by surprise and I too regretted it almost immediately. Why should I talk about my Father to this bastard? What was the use?

At that age I used to explode time and again whenever I heard anti-Semitic taunts. And then... then I became inured. No,

I never became reconciled to the insults, but I realised they were to be part of my life.

When I started writing poetry, Mother introduced me to a prominent poet, who used to teach her at the Literary Institute before the war. After reading my poems he said: 'Not bad... But your name... You will need to change it.' 'Why? What for?' I asked dully. He thought for a moment. 'Well, you must take a Russian surname.' I said I'd think about it and consult my husband. But Boris thought the idea absurd, and so, thank God, I retained my name.

One day in the 1970s I was walking along a noisy street with the poet Vassily Kazin, who was trying to explain to me why my poetry collections invariably got stuck at the publishers. At one point he beckoned to me and whispered into my ear: 'It's your Jewish name. They don't like it.' How pitiful it was to be afraid to say these words out loud in the middle of a noisy street! It was common knowledge anyway. However, my nationality was not the only reason. Books got stuck even when their authors had pure Slavic names — if they were honest books, with no influential hand pushing them along.

Well then, did I feel at home in my country, did I feel I belonged? As a matter of fact I did. The persistent badgering voice was never able to drown out the other voices, which spoke to my heart, loving and loved, habitual and yet shatteringly novel.

The soundtrack of my childhood: the clanging of trams, the monotonous call of the rag and bone man '*Staryo beryom!*' and of the knife-grinder: '*Tochit nozhi-nozhnitsy!*' Their musicality does not, alas, come across in translation. Ditties ringing out to the accompaniment of a sparkling accordion on holidays, Dunayevsky's jaunty songs booming out from loudspeakers, the eternal scales, exercises and easy pieces by Grechaninov and Cerni at my music school. The sickly-sweet smell emanating from the Red October chocolate factory, the Udarnik cinema house, which we, youngsters, regarded as our own and where we never missed a film. It was my city, with its spring ice-floes on the river Moskva, and the vast staircase leading up to the enormous Lenin Library.

Part of my homeland was my school No. 585, and my schoolmates, whom I missed when, in 1952, we moved to another district, and my old literature teacher.

Part of my homeland were the crowded and noisy streets of Kuznetsky Most and Petrovka, so typically Muscovite, where as a teenager I would stroll for hours with friends.

Part of my homeland were the woods off the Severyanin and Yauza suburban stations, and the camp-fires on the river Pra in Meschera country, and the tiny town of Plyos perched on the tall bank of the Volga. Also part of my homeland was the deserted shore of the White Sea, and on its beach the lonely log on which somebody had carved the word 'Paradise'. Northern forests with mosquitoes and cloudberries. Sokolniki park in Moscow, where I went for long ambles with the blue-eyed boy who was my first love.

It has all been ground to dust. Ground by the destruction machine, which was set into motion before I was born and which has not stopped to this day.

I do not mean the Moscow of 'gardens, cobblestones and church bells' described by Marina Tsvetayeva's daughter Ariadna Efron. That Moscow disappeared long before my time. But now they have pulled down my childhood home and the lilacs garden where I used to take my elder boy for walks. The place where they once stood is now a busy thoroughfare dominated by a cast-iron Lenin. Surely this Bolshaya Polyanka could never become part of someone's beloved childhood memory! Or could it? So many districts, neighbourhoods and streets have ceased to exist.

Can I feel at home in a city I once loved which has died before my very eyes? Can I feel at home hearing raucous voices on all sides shouting 'Get back to Israel, Jews! You have ruined Russia!' Feeling today in 1990, just as I did back in 1953, that pogroms could begin at any moment? It is difficult to tell if many people are really out for our blood or if it is only a noisy small mob. But for how long can you tempt fate?

Ever since I can remember I have feared for my dear ones. First for my grandfather, with his typically Jewish face and accent. Now for my children, with their Jewish surname. As a child I was ashamed of my relatives' Jewish names. And today at poetry recitals, I find myself counting the number of Jewish faces and wondering if there are too many of them. Goodness, what paltry, ignoble thoughts! But am I really to blame for them?

It was my not so good fortune to see at arm's length those self-confident, cruel youths from the Russian fascist organisation, called *Pamyat* (Memory). They were wearing black shirts and broad belts, and yelling gleefully: 'This is our land and we are staying! You go, get the hell out of Russia!' And Jews were getting out in their thousands. They are still leaving, leaving their native Russia. But that's nothing new either. Eighteen years ago our friends were leaving Russia for their 'promised homeland', having spent several years of their lives battling against the obtuse state machine. Thus began the exodus. My husband, a civil rights activist, helped them to leave, but neither he nor I ever wanted to leave. I once dreamt that I was wandering about the streets unable to recognise a single face or a single house. Then I realised we were emigrants and woke up in a cold sweat.

In 1978, my best friend, the poet Felix Roziner emigrated. 'I want to write without the censors looking over my shoulder. I refuse to lie.' For almost a year I dialled his number without lifting the receiver.

It was getting harder and harder to breathe. Just as Moscow was disintegrating before our eyes, so was cultural life, never too buoyant anyway. I was born early enough to meet people whose minds were shaped in a different time, for whom Literature, Painting, Music and Human Contact were fundamental, undying values. We would get together at somebody's place to read poetry and discuss books, music, painting.

Cultural life, the embers of which still glowed in the early 70s, was petering out. Among the last 'flickers' of this life were the 'home exhibitions' of 1975, staged by underground artists in their apartments or studios. We felt both frightened and exhilarated as we sought out the secret address, went up in the lift to the 'subversive' apartment or down to the basement to see forbidden canvasses, some of which were true masterpieces. Despite the 'bulldozer attack' on artists at the open-air exhibition in Belayevo, when paintings were crushed under the wheels, art was finding its way to the public, asserting, even through unskilled pictures, that free art was still alive. We felt that the bulldozers would soon be upon us. And so they were. I recall those exhibitions as a bright spring day in the midst of a bitterly frosty winter.

This period of underground culture, with plays, shows, lectures and concerts held in private apartments, was short-lived.

In 1976 we met Peter Starchik, who had recently been discharged from the punitive psychiatric hospital in Kazan where he had been committed for distributing 'anti-Soviet propaganda'. While in hospital, Peter began composing songs to the words of Tsvetayeva, Mandelstam, Bely, Shalamov and lesser-known poets. He sang them at our gatherings to the accompaniment of a guitar. Perhaps his songs lacked professionalism, but they were unforgettable for the tragic emotions and passion they conveyed. In the suffocating dusk of those chilly years he kept up a fire for which we all longed.

But those watchful eyes in the Lubyanka never missed a flame of any kind, not even a candle flickering. They sent their grey firemen, quick and noiseless shadows, to put them out.

One day several of us went to visit yet another home exhibition — of the artist Maxim Dubakh — in a car driven by Peter's brother Alik. Peter persuaded him to stop off at the local police station, where he had been summoned in connection with a complaint coming from his neighbours in the communal apartment. Given that Peter's only neighbours on his ground floor were a family of deaf mutes, the summons was ridiculous. 'It won't take more than five minutes,' Peter told us.

Peter went inside, and the rest of us, my husband Boris and I, Alik, Peter's wife Saida and their children, remained outside in the car. After about half an hour, we decided to go in to inquire. At once a short, muscular individual in a white shirt with rolled-up sleeves came over and said imperviously: 'You're out of bounds. Go and wait downstairs.' Before we had time to move, Peter emerged into the corridor surrounded by several policemen. His face was distraught. The policemen escorted him the length of the corridor and into a room at the end. The muscle-man was joined by another of the same species. They planted themselves across the corridor, pushing us back and repeating: 'Please, go down. You are not allowed to be here. Come on, now! Down!' We went down the stairs and ran to the back door. Outside an ambulance was waiting. It had obviously been called to take Peter away. Soon he appeared with two medical attendants and some senior police officers. His wife and children rushed up to him, while Boris and Alik approached the man, who was obviously in charge: 'Please bear in mind that Academician Sakharov is personally involved in this case. He will report it to Leonid Brezhnev,' Boris said in a loud voice. 'And who might you be?' the man demanded. Boris and Alik were taken upstairs, where some KGB men checked their papers, wrote down their names and addresses, and promised them that their interference would have dire consequences.

In the meantime the attendants, holding Peter by the arms, were leading him towards the ambulance, while Saida and his children clutched at him, holding him back. 'Now, now, Mr Starchik, come on now, come on,' one of the white-coated attendants urged, tugging at him. Finally they succeeded in dragging him away from his weeping wife and children, pushed him into the ambulance and got in themselves. The car started. The children screamed. Saida ran some way after the ambulance, then stopped. She looked ghastly. At the gate a policeman was trying to start his motorcycle. 'You bastard!' she shouted at him, picked up a lump of clay and hurled it at him. He glanced around, and I saw embarrassment on his young face. I was shivering.

We had just witnessed a catastrophe: our friend Peter Starchik had been whisked off to a mental hospital where he would be confined not for days or weeks, but possibly for years, perhaps until his dying day.

During those first weeks Peter managed to smuggle out several short notes, from which we learned that he was confined in a ward which was so overcrowded that you could hardly walk between the beds. The attendants beat up patients under the slightest pretext, and his neighbour seemed to like putting out burning cigarette stubs on Peter's bare arms. Later Peter showed us scars from these burns.

After a while Peter's notes became confused and his writing almost illegible — they had begun the 'treatment'. He told us later that after each injection he salivated and felt violently sick, his mind became dim, his memory failed him, and apathy and listlessness gripped his whole being.

Their aim was to destroy his personality.

Then a miracle happened. The iron grip on him eased. The international campaign launched in his defence proved unexpectedly effective. The injections stopped, Peter was transferred to another ward, where he was even allowed a radio and his guitar. Once he switched on the radio to hear... his own voice singing. He began to wonder if he really had gone round the bend, if he was hearing things. But no, it really was a Western station broadcasting Starchik's songs — about prisons and concentration camps, about the Whites and Reds, about those who had left and those who had stayed, in a word, about Russia and its terrible fate. Those were the very songs that had earned him punishment in a mental hospital.

On 15 November 1976, a car pulled up in front of our house. At the wheel, as on that hapless day, was Alik. But this time we were in for a happy surprise. 'Larissa!' I heard a shout. I ran up to the window and saw Peter standing by the car craning his neck, a sad smile on his face. Saida was beside him. A minute later they were with us. Peter was emaciated and pale. A black overcoat hung ridiculously loose on him. 'They say this coat belonged to Mikhail Chekhov himself, the actor,' Peter said. I hugged him warmly. He seemed dazed by the sudden change in his fortunes. He wandered about the flat distractedly, looked at my younger boy sleeping in his cot and whispered, 'How he's grown!' He obviously couldn't believe that he was free and in his friends' home.

Friends kept coming that day and telephone rang incessantly while Peter sang one song after another, including the songs composed at the hospital. It was then he sang his best song 'The Ballad of a Smoke-filled Carriage' which had just been published in the poetry collection *Poetry Day* that we sent him in the hospital. 'Never part with your beloved...' he sang with Saida singing second part. 'You may be leaving for just a moment but it can turn out to be forever...' The melody evoked a fast rolling train, and the imminent crash. It was a heart-rending song. Everybody had tears in their eyes.

Five years later, a French journalist asked a Soviet official at a press conference: 'Is it true that in your country people get arrested for singing songs in their own homes?' He must have quoted from the petition in defence of Peter Starchik, written by my husband Boris Altschuler.

In the late 1970s the Helsinki group was smashed. Arrests... arrests... arrests... The new decade began with Academician Sakharov's exile. What was happening to the country, everybody asked themselves. But for me there was a more personal question: how would Sakharov's exile affect our family? My husband was his close friend and long-time associate. I had a premonition of those 'dire consequences'. Each day that passed uneventfully seemed a miracle.

In March 1982, I was summoned to the Lubyanka. 'Your husband Boris Altschuler has been lying to you,' said the investigator, a young man with a crew cut. 'His connection with the Academician (he never actually pronounced the dreaded name Sakharov) has not been scientific at all. He has been involved with him in anti-Soviet activities. You have two alternatives: either leave the country within two weeks, or...' he paused, meaningfully, '...or your husband will not see his children for the next ten to fifteen years.' He articulated these words clearly and with obvious enjoyment. 'Is there no third alternative?' I asked dully, having listened to him wordlessly until that moment. The investigator burst into happy laughter. 'Be grateful that you have any alternatives at all,' he said.

In May I saw the same investigator again, but this time he said bluntly: 'Forget about leaving the country. That was just a tactic — to test your reactions. You will never be allowed to leave. You'd better explain to your husband that he has one last chance. If he doesn't listen to this warning he will have only himself to blame.' It is difficult to say what they had hoped to achieve by their 'tactic' and their 'test'. That spring Boris lost his job at the research institute and it took him several months to find another. The only job he could find was a janitor on the neighbouring housing estate.

November 17, 1983. Nine o'clock in the morning. A knock at the door. 'Who's there?' I asked. A voice said they were from the housing management. When I opened the door, eight burly men pushed their way in. 'Burglars!' I decided and tried to stop them closing the door. Then one of them showed me his I.D. I couldn't understand a single word on it, but knew it was the KGB. 'They are going to search your flat,' the man said. 'I have to go!' I protested naively. 'I have an appointment. I must at least telephone and tell them I am not coming.' I grabbed the receiver, but one of the men clamped his hand on the cradle. 'No calls. Are you alone in the flat?' 'The children are here.' 'Wake them up.' I aroused the children. They dressed quickly and watched. Somehow I managed to talk the chief into letting the elder boy go to school. My son understood my sign to him and ran to his father who was sweeping the yard nearby. Boris was able to call some people and to pass his diary into reliable hands. Then he came home. Soon Alik appeared, followed by our friend the writer Yuri Karabchiyevsky. Both were immediately subjected to an interrogation (name, relationship to us, purpose of visit). Yuri knew he would not be allowed to leave until the search was over and the purpose of his visit was to help us live through that interminable day. His presence, his lively conversation and his jokes did help to cheer us up. The search lasted until evening. 'Will they take him away?' was the thought that hammered my brain all those hours.

I watched listlessly as the eight men rummaged through our belongings, books, manuscripts, diaries, lifted the desk calendar with my jottings off its stand and packed it away. But when I went out into the hall and saw one of the men reading a rough draft of my poem he had fished out of my coat, I yelled: 'How dare you? I don't even show my drafts to my husband!'

They took away a pile of books: Mandelstam, Nabokov, Tsvetayeva, a typewritten copy of Felix Roziner's novel *A Certain Finkelmeier*, three typewriters, cassettes with classical music, English recordings and songs by Felix and Peter.

The country was stagnating. It was pointless reading periodicals, listening to the radio, watching television, going to the theatre. A living person was a *persona non grata* in a country ruled by dead men, who held it in their grip, destroying any manifestation of life.

How did we manage to hold on to life? Well, we clung to things we could trust — family, friends, books, music, memory, folk wisdom accumulated over the ages, and nature, ravished and defiled, but nevertheless beautiful.

The eighties were a grim, hopeless decade.

Then suddenly a new age dawned, the era of shattering glasnost, belated confessions, accusations, self-flagellations and words... words... words... It was an avalanche of words, which seemed unimaginably candid, repentant, terrible and superficial.

A wave of disasters swept through the country: Chernobyl, Karabakh... people with radiation disease, cripples, refugees, victims of brutal, primeval ethnic hatred — all these surfaced. The reality was getting nightmarish. All at once every lever and brake failed, and all the bolts which held life together, were wrenched out, threading and all. Silence disappeared. And not only silence, but your inner right to it. One could no longer hide in a corner and live in opposition to the regime. Not in this feverish hysterical upside-down world where problems kept piling up and were never resolved, in which old crimes were divulged and new ones committed, in which old wounds were exposed for all to see, and fresh ones were carefully concealed. Tragedy acquired the quality of farce. That which had been forbidden or persecuted was now in demand. Life as such became superfluous. The simple things of life were no longer relevant.

As I stepped, or, rather, flew across the state border, I made many discoveries. The three most important ones were: the mythical, mysterious 'abroad' really existed. Second, it consists of many different countries. Third, they are brightly-coloured and festive. Their citizens live, they don't just drag out an existence. The people are friendly and polite to one another. The shops are full of goods, and the problems, however serious, are not deadly, because they are problems of life and not of survival.

In lieu of Conclusion

Everything passes with time: the man and the age. Another age arrives, and another man. Yet he, like his predecessor, is bound to start reflecting on his relationship with TIME and SPACE. Past, present, future — what do we know of them? Do we know more about the past than the future? 'The leisurely pace of the good old days', I read in someone's memoirs. But were they really leisurely and good? Or is that an illusion? What does 'old' mean anyway? And won't the frantic pace of life today seem moderate and calm tomorrow? Yet remembering my childhood I cannot help thinking about it in the same words: 'The leisurely pace of the good old days.' The long winter evenings, the fringed lampshade over the table where Granny was darning, Grandfather was reading the paper, and I was drawing. 'It's quiet, so blessedly quiet that you can hear time flowing past.' And so it flowed leisurely and smoothly. I swam in it leisurely and smoothly.

Each of us, when we are born, falls into the river of time and swims with the stream, rejoicing at everything we find on the way, until one day we suddenly stop and ask ourselves: 'Who am I? Where am I going? Can I touch the bottom?' Once you have asked this, you begin to flounder and sink. You stop swimming like a fish in the river of time and have to learn to swim again, which may take the rest of your life.

'Row, row, row your boat gently down the stream, merrily, merrily, merrily, life is but a dream', says the old English folk song. It is normally sung as a round, with people coming in one after the other, the same way you enter the river of time. Only, alas, few of us manage to swim along this stream 'gently and merrily'. It is hard to accept the fact that 'life is but a dream', in which nothing exists except deceptive ideas about deceptive things and that if you say 'I know' today, you may realise tomorrow that you were mistaken.

A friend of ours who emigrated to the States in the early seventies complained to an American colleague: 'The trouble is I can't get to work without a car, but I don't like driving. It makes things very difficult. I have a most complicated relationship with my car. I don't know what to do.' 'I think you must change your attitude,' the sensible American advised him. 'Change your attitude,' I have repeated to myself hundreds of times when I found myself in a no-win situation. Change your attitude to the deceptive, fickle world where changing illusions is as natural and unavoidable as the changing seasons. Change the accent, shift the emphasis from vain hopes to vain despair. What you call a change of mirages could just as well be termed a transformation, something that turns each new day into a tabula rasa. So swim without fear or hesitation. Swim until time drifts into eternity and you into oblivion. Yet who knows where time will drift and what will happen beyond the bounds of this earthly life.

* * *

Diversity of grass and flowers!
Go catch them in the leisure hour
In rain or sun net — and be rich!
I catch them in my word net...which
Is why they're very hard to capture
And all too often they flit past you
So once more you've an empty net,
No grass or petal in it yet.
But my wish is that when it's chilly
I still may see a flowering lily,
That every moment of delight
Should stay, not vanish from my sight.
That fair June days and nights star-spangled
In my fair net of words entangled
Should gladden with their warmth sublime
The very dead of wintertime;
That every one now seen or seeing,
Now singing songs of joy or weeping,
All who tomorrow shall be gone
Should in my poetry live on.

* * *

Time passes relentlessly,
Joy and sorrow.
What is here today
Will be gone tomorrow.
Yet a distant glimmer
Gives hope and sustains.
And on we swim, cursing fate,
As the days pass by,
Vanitas vanitatum, they slip away,
Fickle and fleeting,
Yet we forget that only this way,
Tried and tested, can grant us a ray,
A taste of the light
That gleaming is shed
In the darkness that lies ahead.

Translated by Peter Tempest

BACK ISSUES OF GLAS:

Revolution, the 1920s and 1980s

Soviet Grotesque, young people's rebellion against the establishment

Women's View, Russian woman bloodied but unbowed

Love and Fear, the two strongest emotions dominating Russian life

Bulgakov & Mandelstam, earlier autobiographical stories

Jews & Strangers, what it means to be a Jew in Russia

Booker Winners & Others, mostly provincial writers

Love Russian Style, Russia tries decadence

The Scared Generation, the grim background of today's ruling class

Booker Winners & Others-II, more samplings from the Booker winners

Captives, victors turn out to be captives on conquered territory

From Three Worlds, new Ukrainian writing

A Will & a Way, new women's writing

Beyond the Looking-Glas, Russian grotesque revisited

Peter Aleshkovsky, *Skunk: A Life*, a novel set in the Russian countryside

Chilldhood, the child is father to the man

Ludmila Ulitskaya, *Sonechka*, a novel about a persevering woman

Asar Eppel, *The Grassy Street*, stories set in a Moscow suburb in the 1940s

Boris Slutsky, *Things That Happend*, the poetry & biography of a major poet

The Portable Platonov, for the centenary of Russia's greatest writer

Leonid Latynin, *The Face-Maker and the Muse*, a novel-parable

Irina Muravyova, *The Nomadic Soul*, a novel about modern Anna Karenina

Anatoly Mariengof, *A Novel Without Lies*, a story of a great poet

Alexander Genis, *Red Bread,* comparative portrayals of Russia and America

"The writing in Glas offers startling evidence that the great Russian literary tradition lives on." —
AMERICAN BOOKSELLER